Long Ago and Far Away

Remembering Vietnam Fifty Years On

BY ROBERT K. GRIFFITH JR.

The contents of this work, including, but not limited to, the accuracy of events, people, and places depicted; opinions expressed; permission to use previously published materials included; and any advice given or actions advocated are solely the responsibility of the author, who assumes all liability for said work and indemnifies the publisher against any claims stemming from publication of the work.

All Rights Reserved
Copyright © 2022 by Robert K. Griffith Jr.

No part of this book may be reproduced or transmitted, downloaded, distributed, reverse engineered, or stored in or introduced into any information storage and retrieval system, in any form or by any means, including photocopying and recording, whether electronic or mechanical, now known or hereinafter invented without permission in writing from the publisher.

Dorrance Publishing Co
585 Alpha Drive
Pittsburgh, PA 15238
Visit our website at *www.dorrancebookstore.com*

ISBN: 978-1-6386-7344-6
ESIBN: 978-1-6386-7347-7

About the Author

Robert Griffith retired as the chief of strategic planning for the State of Rhode Island in 2014. He served in the Army from 1967 to 1987. He taught History at the United States Military Academy, history and politics at the U.S. Army Command and General Staff College, and the Industrial College of the Armed Forces, National Defense University. He also served as a military author at the Army's Center of Military History. As a combat arms officer, he served in Armor and Armored Cavalry units in the United States, Germany, and Vietnam. He is a decorated combat veteran.

He is the author of *The U.S. Army's Transition to the All-Volunteer Force, 1968-1974* and *Men Wanted for the U.S. Army: America's Experience with an All-Volunteer Army Between the World Wars* and several articles on the history of American military manpower systems. In 1992, Griffith joined a special commission appointed by the secretary of the army to investigate why no Black soldiers were awarded the Medal of Honor in WWII. As a result of the commission's efforts, seven Black veterans received the Congressional Medal of Honor, six posthumously and one still living.

Dr. Griffith received his undergraduate training at the U.S. Military Academy and an M.A. and Ph.D. in History from Brown University. He was also a recipient of a postdoctoral Congressional Fellowship from the American Political Science Association.

Fifty years on, Vietnam veteran Robert Griffith tells the story of *his* war. This is a work of remembrance: of war in its day-to-day details, of combat and camaraderie, of how, in 1968, a young officer in 3/5 Cav sought to find out whether he was "cut out for war." It is also a work of reconstruction, as the military historian that young army officer became pieces together the history he lived and lays to rest some of the shadows of his war.

Beth Bailey
Author of *America's Army: Making the All-Volunteer Force*

America's Vietnam War may today seem Long Ago and Far Away in time and space. But Robert Griffith's vividly written memoir of his service in Vietnam possesses a gripping immediacy, laced with flashes of humor and enduring lessons in leadership. It is an important contribution to the literature of that war.

Andrew Bacevich, author of America's War for the Greater Middle East: A Military History.

For Johana

Introduction

This book began in my head long before I started to write it down. In the first years after my service in Vietnam, I was too busy getting on with my life as an army officer, husband, and father to pay it much attention. It would crop up in my mind occasionally, when something happened there, like the Easter Offensive in 1972 or the ultimate victory of the North over South Vietnam in 1975. Lyndon Johnson's death in January 1973, when I was in graduate school, also proved to be a time for reflection on the war.

On active duty and teaching American History at West Point did not lead me to think deeply about the war. All of us officers spent at least one tour of duty there. We could read each other's histories written on the unit patches on our shoulders, branch insignia on our lapels and ribbons on our chests. When we did talk about our experiences in the war, the conversation was about its rightness or wrongness, its battles, its tactics and strategy, its policy and politics. As a budding historian, I had been taught to avoid generalizing from personal experience.

My time as an author at the Army's Center of Military History and on the faculties of the Army Command and General Staff College and the National Defense University's Industrial College of the Armed Forces, now known as the Eisenhower School of National Security and Resources Strategy, coincided with the "Long Peace" between Vietnam and the United States' military rebuilding for what became the last phase of the Cold War. Focus on preparing for the Air Land Battle left little time or interest in national wars of liberation.

After I retired from military service, I began to think about my Vietnam experiences more often. When the First Gulf War erupted in February 1990, memories of *my war* intruded more frequently. I could not bring myself to get caught up in the patriotic fervor that gripped friends and neighbors as they followed the nation's mobilization and deployment for war in the Mid-East. Instead, my thoughts returned to my own naivete as friends and I prepared and trained for the U.S. Army's role in the war in Vietnam.

I did not have any trouble remembering my experiences in Vietnam. I did have a compelling need for more context. I had a rather good grounding in the geopolitical basis of the war and in the broad critique of its conduct. I wanted to know about the soldiers' war. For years I had studied the experiences of the American, British, French and German authors of the Great War. As I read the memoirs of the survivors of Vietnam, I began to see similarities. The WWI generation and ours shared not only the privations and horrors of war, but the disillusionment and sense of futility of the war and peace that followed as well. That is when I began to integrate my own experience into the mix of Vietnam memoirs.

As the fiftieth anniversary of the end of U.S. involvement approached, I began to dwell on my experience soldiering in Vietnam. I concluded that my war was not that different from those of most others. I experienced the privations, fear, and boredom like most. Like most, I also saw the humor, absurdities, and irony. Most of all, I shared in the camaraderie between men thrown together in trying circumstances and working to keep themselves and each other alive while maintaining their sense of humanity. I did not want to forget them.

I was lucky. Reconstructing my experience started with my letters home. My parents and fiancé saved all my letters. Rereading them helped me remember events, people, places, and how they fit together in time. My next step involved reconnecting with some of the men with whom I served. They in turn introduced me to the veterans association of my Vietnam unit. I started attending its biennial reunions. That brought me two additional resources, reconnections with more brothers-in-arms and a research trove of documents from the war. The internet also proved to be valuable. Through it I got in touch with men from other units who participated in the same activities and battles as we did. Occasionally this led to documents that corroborated or corrected my interpretation and understanding of events. Another source is the Vietnam Center & Sam Johnson Vietnam Archive (VNCA) at Texas Tech University. From its virtual archive I was able to locate pertinent documents not available in the Black Knights Association website. I would be remiss if I did not mention what a source Wikipedia is. In graduate school and as a teacher we discouraged its use. Today its entries are peer reviewed. Its coverage of the Vietnam war is extensive.

I have many people to thank for enabling me to bring this work to fruition. They include Dr. Josh Berger, VMAC Providence, who helped me through some of the rough spots in my memory, Barry Goree, Rick Hoban, Dave Meaders, Terry Reigle and Peter Walker who provided information about my time in the Cavalry and answered questions about people and events. Archivists at The Black Knights, 3rd Squadron, 5th U.S. Cavalry Vietnam Veterans Association also helped, as did the Vietnam Center & Sam Johnson Vietnam Archive (VNCA). Larry Gwin, author of *Baptism, A Combat Memoir of Vietnam*, Harry Rothman, senior editor of RCI Publications, who read early versions of my manuscript, and Benjamin Altomari, Rachael Bindas and Maisi McIntyre of Dorrance Publishing who shepherded it through the publishing process. Thanks also to my family; Maria Griffith, an English writing teacher, who did the initial editing, Rob and his wife Christine, and Anne Griffith for their curiosity, patience and tolerance. Finally, my sincerest thanks to my wife Johana who has now been through my war in Vietnam twice and to whom this work is dedicated.

Chapter One
Preparations

I volunteered. It seemed like a good idea at the time. It is an old story. In the spring of 1967, we were to select our branch and first assignments. The war was going big time. There was no doubt that it would not be over before we got our chance. I thought of it as graduate school. Four years at West Point prepared me, or so I thought, to be an officer, and what better way to find out whether those four years of training were satisfactory. As one of my mentors, a major ten years my senior put it, it was better that I find out early in my career whether I was cut out for war rather than wait ten years in his case. I already had selected armor as my basic branch, armored cavalry as my specialty.

So, there we were in a computer lab in the bowels of Thayer Hall with a couple of armor officers strutting up and down the platform exhorting us to make the most of the opportunity to find out what war was all about, get over there and get some metals on your chest, or, in the words of Pres. Lyndon Johnson "nail the coonskin to the wall." When my turn came, I proudly selected the 11th Armored Cavalry Regiment.

Upon graduation, I enjoyed sixty days' leave, mostly at home in Massachusetts and mostly with Johana, my fiancé. We took in Expo '67 in Montreal and drove through the Canadian Maritimes camping at Ingonish on Cape Breton Island. Then I headed to Fort Benning, Georgia for nine weeks of Ranger training.

As I headed south from Atlanta in my red Austin Healy with New York plates, I half expected Rod Steiger to pop up from behind a billboard and pull me over. The movie *In the Heat of the Night* was then playing and once I got off the interstate, I was sure I was fresh fish for the local constabulary. I arrived safely and without incident at Fort Benning and was quickly ushered into the world of the Rangers.

Ranger School was everything it was cracked up to be. Under tactical conditions we received small unit training in the mountains of northern Georgia and swamps of Florida. Kept constantly on the move, deprived of food and sleep, the program instilled skills and confidence that prepared us for duty in Vietnam.

Nine weeks later, several pounds lighter, physically harder than I had ever been and seriously hungry I completed Ranger School. This was not without incident, and I still marvel at the fact that I successfully completed the program. On one occasion trying to evade capture during a night ambush I rolled off a cliff and hung up in a tree. When I woke in the morning, I found that I had lost my weapon, that I had secured to my web gear with a boot lace. Slithering down the tree I began looking for the weapon when I heard a scuffling sound and turned to see a mother black bear and two cubs. With a snort, she sent the cubs up a nearby tree and turned menacingly in my direction. I backed slowly away and, when I had gone what seemed to be a safe distance, turned and ran. I never did find the weapon.

On another occasion, the last night before graduation, we made a forced march of several miles and took up a blocking position in an open field. Exhausted, I dozed off. I awoke with a start thinking we were being attacked and started firing the M60 machine gun that I had been issued for the exercise, blanks of course. Now fully awake and aware of what I had done I was sure I had blown it. Somehow the fates took pity on me and after a return forced march to the training area, I received the coveted tab.

Those of us who were armor officers made a quick departure from Fort Benning and headed for Fort Knox, Kentucky where we were to attend an abbreviated six-week armor officer basic course. First a couple of classmates and I checked into a Holiday Inn for some serious sleep and hot baths. I got the tub first because I was a Red Sox fan and the "impossible dream" team was in the series. The next day the three of us headed for Kentucky backtracking the route Sherman had taken to Atlanta. We also toured the Chickamauga and Chattanooga battlefields.

The Armor Officer Basic Course proved to be something of a disappointment to me. By the fall of 1967, tank and armored cavalry units had been in Vietnam for almost two years. The course however was more oriented toward conventional armored warfare on the plains of Western Europe. Little if any attention was paid to the kinds of operations and tactics being developed extemporaneously by cavalry and armored units fighting a real war in Southeast Asia.

Fort Knox was not a total loss. About halfway through the course, Jo was able to join me for an extended weekend. We enjoyed a wonderful weekend. We had not seen each other since I left for Ranger School in August. We took in the sights around Knox and partied with friends. We stayed with my classmate Gary Carlson and his wife Donna (Gary died in Vietnam).

My other diversion during that time was rally racing. Several of us joined a local sports car rally club and competed on the side and back roads of Kentucky on weekends. Rallying involved skills like map reading on the move and keeping time on a prescribed course rather than speed. Once, trying to make up time, I came into a check point sideways and stove in the right rear fender of my precious Austin Healy.

My next stop was Fort Meade, Maryland where I was to spend approximately six months as a platoon leader with the Sixth Armored Cavalry Regiment. The logic of this assignment was to provide newly commissioned officers practical experience leading troops in a non-hostile environment. This proved to be something of a mixed bag. The regiment had just completed its annual training cycle. Thus, the first month or so of my assignment as a platoon leader was largely administrative in nature. As winter turned to spring in 1968, we began doing riot control training in anticipation of a return to Washington of antiwar protesters who in the previous year had surrounded the Pentagon and attempted to levitate it. My boredom was broken by occasional weekend sorties to New York to spend time with Jo, who was in college there. She in turn came to Ft. Meade as often as possible.

During my assignment to the Sixth Cavalry two events occurred that brought the reality of the war in Vietnam clearly into focus. In preparation for the annual West Point "Founders Day" dinner, I, along with other lieutenant graduates of the academy, was detailed to set up the venue for the event. This involved hanging plaques listing the names of West Pointers killed in Vietnam. I was dumbfounded to see the name of my first "Beast Barracks" squad leader, Robert Keats, on the list. Bob was two years my senior and we had become friends. He was the first person I knew to fall in the war.

The second event involving the war came in a letter from a brother officer who had recently transferred to an armor unit in Vietnam. Like me, he had been assigned to the Sixth to gain experience leading troops prior to deployment. The tone of the letter was casual except for the news that he had been wounded during one of his first missions. This news, especially the "oh, by the way," manner it was delivered, brought all of us lieutenants up short.

One of the many things I learned during that period was how to get along with Non-Commissioned Officers (NCOs), especially senior NCOs. My platoon sergeant, a German named Hoffer, had no use for me. It was his platoon before I arrived, and my orders for Vietnam foretold my departure in only six months when it would be his platoon again. Then in February I was assigned paymaster for the troop. Accompanied by an armed guard I went to the post finance office, counted out $250,000.00 in cash, broke it down into individual amounts and returned to the troop where I dispensed it to the soldiers. After that I returned to the finance office and turned in the paid vouchers and cash for the soldiers not present. Every penny paid out and left over had to balance exactly with the amount I had drawn originally.

While I was completing my paymaster duties the enlisted men had the rest of the day off to pay bills or spend their cash blowing off steam at a favored bar or heading to "The Block," Baltimore's notorious Red-Light District. Sometime after 10:00 PM, I was awakened by a call from the local constabulary and invited to come down to the town jail and retrieve platoon sergeant (PSG) Hoffer from the drunk tank. I did so, took him back to his barracks and saw him to bed. The next morning, he presented himself to me in his best uniform, with a chagrined look on his face and a hangover so obvious that my head ached. He swore it would never happen again. I told him he was correct and that we would never speak of it again. After that I could do no wrong, and we settled into a comfortable and professional relationship. He counselled me in the role and art of the platoon leader and helped prepare me for the many challenges ahead.

Dr. Martin Luther King's assassination in April changed all that. The Sixth along with other Regular Army units around Washington was quickly called up and brought into the city to impose order and protect property as the grief and anger over King's murder quickly spread to the streets and turned violent. It was one of those weekends that Jo was coming to Meade; she pulled into the main gate while we moved out the South Gate on our way to DC.

My platoon of forty men occupied ten blocks of 14th St. I had one Jeep and two radios to keep up with my assigned area. It was here that I heard my first shots fired in anger. Several rioters had entered an automobile dealership and were looting it when a store employee appeared and fired on them. They of course were also armed, and a brief firefight occurred. The next day when it became warmer, entire families showed up to protest, some to selectively loot local clothing stores. I took a squad into the store to chase them out. I moved toward the back of the store and got cut off by the crowd from my men. Truly scared I managed to extricate myself safely. Then we were ordered to clear 14th Street and used our riot control training to do just that. Taking up a wedge formation and employing ample teargas we advanced up 14th St., breaking the large crowds into smaller groups and sealing them off on the side streets. It was here that I learned my second lesson.

Even before King's assassination race relations in the United States had become increasingly strained. Blacks, especially Black youths, in the country supported by northern white college students and liberal members of the middle class lost patience with establishment platitudes about gradualism and began to aggressively advocate for change. The armed services proudly pointed to its record of desegregation since President Truman ordered it by Executive Order 9981 in 1948. Young Blacks in the military were increasingly unimpressed and shared the views of their activist brothers. They saw no reason why they should be restraining the rioters. This attitude in turn infuriated some of the older senior Black NCOs, many of whom had enlisted before and during WWII when the army was strictly "Jim Crow." They had seen the progress since 1948 and did not want a bunch of hot head "bucks" messing up the good they had achieved. The "brothers" in turn saw the older Black NCOs as a bunch of "Uncle Toms" and challenged their legitimacy. This threatened the very fabric of the leadership structure of the enlisted ranks. White officers, especially young white officers found themselves caught in the middle of this long-simmering issue which they ignored to their peril.

We remained in Washington for the duration of April and into May. I was detached and sent to Ft. Story on the coast of Chesapeake, Virginia for special training in how to compose and send encrypted messages in the event I became a prisoner of war. We students were paired with a "familiar" correspondent with whom we exchanged letters. I did so, but after arriving in Vietnam soon lost contact. The assignment to Ft. Story was idyllic. My temporary quarters were a beach cottage on the coast. I took most of my meals at a navy "closed mess" where we were served on linin tablecloths and receive wine with dinner. This was a totally new experience that I did not encounter again until I served in Vietnam.

After my brief assignment to Ft. Story, I returned to the Sixth Cavalry. My six months troop duty came to an end. After about a week's leave at home (to put my affairs in order?) I kissed my sweetheart good buy; my brother Lou took me to Logan Airport, and I headed west to Travis Air Force Base California. The next day a commercial airliner headed to Vietnam.

Chapter Two
Welcome to 3rd Squadron, 5th Cavalry

I arrived in Vietnam pretty much the same way everyone else did, via contract commercial airliner from Travis Air Force Base to Ton Son Nhut airbase. Leaving cruising altitude, we went into a steep descent winding down through clouds for a quick landing. Descent and landing gave us a good look at the pock marked jungle and rice paddies around Saigon. On deplaning we received the clichéd welcome from troops waiting to go home on our plane as soon as we were off it; jeers, cat calls and shouts of, "you'll be sorree"! Loaded on to cattle car like trucks, we were quickly taken to the 90th Replacement Battalion at Long Bien for in-processing, orientation and transportation to our assigned units. In-processing was standard Army stuff; the Army's version of Vietnam history, culture and why we were there. We stood in a lot of lines receiving our tropical fatigues, jungle boots and boonie hats. This was also a time to adjust to the climate. Suffice it to say it was hot and humid. The saving grace of the 90th was the officers club which served drinks for $0.25 a shot. It was here that I had my first run in with the rule "the needs of the army take precedence." My orders stated that I was to be assigned to the 11th Armored Cavalry Regiment. The assignment officer at 90th Replacement said I was going to the Ninth Infantry Division. The 9th had suffered several casualties recently and needed replacement lieutenants. No amount of argument or pleading changed the assignment officer's decision. Shortly thereafter I found myself in another truck going to the headquarters of the 9th at Bearcat. Again, as a result of pleading and arguing, the assignments officer of the 9th took pity on me and assigned me to the division's cavalry squadron.

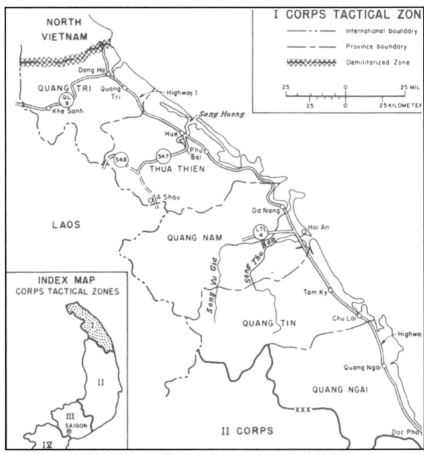

I Corps Tactical Zone. Source: CMH Pub 90-24,
The War in the Northern Provinces, 1966-1968 (1975)

The only problem was that the Third Squadron Fifth Cavalry minus its air cavalry troop was far to the north. Following the Tet Offensive, General Westmorland, concerned about the lack of armored forces in the northern region of Vietnam, ordered 3/5 Cav from III Corps to I Corps to fill the gap. Thus, I hung around D Troop's base camp at Bearcat until the next logistics run to the north was scheduled. Not a bad thing all-in-all as D Troop's bar was even cheaper than the one at Long Bien.

When it came a couple of days later, the logistics run consisted of several enlisted men, mail, spare parts, and a couple of Army of the Republic of Vietnam (ARVN) officers, their families and personal baggage including chickens and a couple of pigs, and me. We all piled aboard a C 130 and were on our way. The flight lasted about four hours. In-flight entertainment was provided by the Vietnamese family members, their chickens and pigs. Every time the plane changed course or altitude, they became extremely agitated and began crying and moaning. No amount of consolation by the ARVN officers could calm them down.

We landed at Phu Bai, a little south and west of Hue. Told that it was too late in the day to complete the journey to 3/5 Cav's base camp, we were put up for the night by a tank company of the Second Battalion 34th Armor that provided road, bridge and base security for Phu Bai.

Next morning after engineers swept the road linking Phu Bai to QL1, the main North-South highway in Vietnam for mines, we departed in a hastily thrown together convoy of trucks and jeeps all heading north. We wound down the hilly piedmont and joined local traffic on QL1 a largely dirt highway interspersed with occasional stretches of asphalt. Coming into the old imperial city we passed the cathedral that clearly showed damage from the recent Tet Offensive. A little further on we came to the Perfume River. Our way across was blocked by a fallen traffic bridge. Vehicle traffic was diverted west to a railroad bridge that had survived attempts by the NVA/VC forces to blow it up when they occupied the city. We moved beyond Hue and followed QL1 about 50 km further north past villages spaced five to ten kilometers apart. These were largely local commercial centers serving agricultural and fishing villages further to the east. From the truck I could see clear to the South China Sea. Any growth along the highway had been cleared with chemicals (Agent Orange) to prevent the enemy from firing on convoys. Sometimes we would get a close look at the peasant rice farmers working in the paddies. Very bucolic, until you looked closer.

The villages along the highway showed signs of recent battle damage. Few shops were open and there was no evidence that schools were open. Most of the larger towns' police stations or army compounds showed heavy damage. Many of the bridges that took the highway over rivers and stream were destroyed; now replaced by temporary prefabricated structures guarded on either side by tanks of the 2/34 Armor reinforced with a few infantrymen. Refugees made up another component of the local population. These people, displaced by fighting in and around Hue and areas further north, lived in crowded shanty towns made of flimsy plywood or woven mats covered with corrugated metal roofs. Some refugees lived in abandoned box cars on the southern bank of the O Gang River near My Chan.

When our little convoy reached the district capital of Hai Lang our truck peeled off to the east and headed to 3/5 Cav's base camp at Wunder Beach.

Wunder Beach was a logistics and supply base built in March 1968 in support of army operations to relieve the besieged 1st Cavalry Division at Khe Sanh. Up until that time support for units in the north flowed through the Navy supply base at Qua Viet. Increased activity south of the DMZ aimed at relieving the siege of Khe Sanh to the west drew the attention of North Vietnamese artillery in the DMZ. Wunder Beach was out of range. Third Squadron Fifth Cavalry was sent to Wunder Beach in early May 1968 to provide base and road security as well as assist engineer units in clearing areas along the desert-like terrain between the South China Sea and the QL1 from Hue to the DMZ.

"Sky King Highway" was an improved dirt road, packed gravel and clay with some drainage. It carried fuel tankers and supply convoys from Wunder Beach through Hai Lang and on to the north where they served army and marine units below the DMZ. To our left and right the land was flat and lush rice farming country. The farmers lived in compact villages of mat and daube walls with dirt floors and thatched roofs. Electric and communication lines were noticeably absent. The peasants, men, women and older children worked the paddies from dawn to dusk returning to their villages at night.

About ten kilometers on we crossed a pontoon bridge into what was once a village. The peasant dwellings were gone; what remained was a Catholic church, its rectory and a school building dating to the time of French colonialism. This was LZ Hard Core. It was occupied by a 105mm artillery battery, some elements of a 3/5 Cavalry troop and a unit of the 1st Cavalry Division. One of the soldiers on the truck told me this was "Street Without Joy" territory, a much fought over area during the French-Indochina War chronicled in the book of the same name by Bernard Fall.

Slowing only to avoid pedestrians and dodge traffic from the Beach, we moved on. The terrain changed dramatically. Passing over a local road, Rt 555, the actual Street Without Joy, and through a prominent North-South sand dune "The Cut" we broke into what could only be described a desert. This area, consisting of largely uninhabited territory of shifting sand and scrub pine crisscrossed by footpaths and interspersed with cemeteries and intermittent brackish ponds, was known as "The Dunes." Another ten kilometers brought us to Wunder Beach. Surrounded by triple concertina razor wire guarded by manned watch towers. It looked formidable.

The truck dropped me off at Squadron Headquarters where I briefly met with the Adjutant to turn in my orders and personal file and the surgeon who took my medical file and asked about my preferred alcohol, I was put up in a spare tent for the night. I was to meet the Squadron Commander in the morning.

Squadron Headquarters consisted of several medium field tents that housed the staff and support troops, mess, supply, maintenance and communications elements and a reconnaissance section. The tent village was situated in a grove of pine trees one barrier dune back from the coast. Although extremely hot, it enjoyed a sea breeze; the trees provided some relief from the almost blinding sun. Looking out over the now dark South China Sea I noticed numerous lights bobbing in the swells of the water. These I was told were fishermen. They lived in villages, not unlike those of the rice farmers, just behind the barrier dunes. During the day they hauled their boats out onto the beach and spent their time mending nets and gear or taking their catch to market.

Tired from a long day rattling along the route from Phu Bai to Wunder Beach I turned in knowing that the morning would bring my real introduction to 3/5 Cavalry.

When Kipling wrote in "Mandalay", "the dawn comes up like thunder outer China 'crost the Bay!", he just as easily could have been speaking about dawn on the South China Sea coast of Vietnam. The sun burst through the flaps of the tent; it was bright and hot immediately, and I was fully awake instantly. I shaved and pulled on my best new-guy fatigues and headed for the mess tent. The squadron commander, a lieutenant colonel greeted me, sat me down at his table, got me a cup of strong black coffee and pastry, and proceeded to brief me on the squadron's mission. He then walked me through the tactical operations center (TOC) introducing me to the operations staff and gave me a map reconnaissance of the squadron's area of operations (AO). Finally, he took me up in his helicopter and had the pilot fly over the entire AO, showing me where the three line troops were located and briefing me on their missions. After returning to squadron headquarters (HQ) and more coffee' he said he was assigning me to A Troop and had his driver take me to A Troop HQ. They were expecting me. The 1st Sergeant (aka Top) told me that my gear had been sent over earlier that morning. It was in the Orderly Room, another medium size tent. When the troop commander and two of the platoons returned from the day's operations, "Dapper SIX", the commander's radio call sign, would decide what to do with me.

I hung around the orderly room making small talk with the clerks and studying maps. Around 17:00 hours I heard the rumble and screech of tanks and the purr of troop carriers as A Troop came in for the night. Top took me over to the Troop Commander's tent that doubled as a meeting room and made introductions. The CO, a tall, sandy haired captain said, "Call me Mac," and tossed me a beer. He in turn introduced the 1st and 2nd Platoon Leaders; 3rd Platoon was at LZ Hard Core. First Platoon was led by a first lieutenant who would shortly move up to troop executive officer. The 2nd Platoon Leader was something of a surprise. He was an NCO of medium height, kind of scruffy, wearing fatigue pants cut off below his knees. He looked like the war comic book character Sergeant Rock. Ironically, his name was Block and he came with a German Shepherd named Bozo. CPT Mac decided to assign me to 1st Platoon. I was to shadow the incumbent platoon leader for a couple of days getting to know the men and a feel for how the platoon fit in with the greater scheme of things.

Sergeant Block and Bozo

The standard armored cavalry platoon in Vietnam consisted of ten vehicles and about forty men. Each platoon was made up of a scout section with four vehicles, an infantry squad in one vehicle, a tank section with three tanks and a mortar section in one vehicle overseen by the platoon leader in one vehicle.

All vehicles except the tanks were modified M113 armored personnel carriers (APC). Originally designed as a troop carrier powered by a 215HP diesel engine, protected by a cold rolled aluminum, manganese and magnesium hull armed with a .50 caliber machine gun mounted in an exposed ring turret on its top. The M113 was deemed "the best land vehicle developed by the United States."[1] By 1967 when 3/5 Cavalry arrived in Vietnam the M113 APC had evolved into the M113 ACAV based on the innovation and experience of the ARVN armored cavalry units that initially received them. First, a wrap-around armored shield was added to protect the .50-Cal. machine gun. Side mounted 7.62 mm machine guns also protected by fabricated ballistic shields further increased the fire power of the ACAV. These M60 machine guns could be dismounted, and ground mounted to provide protection between the tracks or to augment the firepower of infantry advancing in an assault. Additionally, all ACAVs were stripped of the seats intended for carrying troops to battle. This freed the interior to hold more ammunition, usually stacked two ammo boxes deep, other equipment and personnel gear. The infantry squad and mortar section M113s were similarly modified. The mortar section carried a dismountable 4.2-inch mortar and ammunition as well as machine gun ammunition and personal gear in another version of the M113, designated the M106. All crew members rode on top of their ACAV.

The tank section of the armored cavalry platoon rounded out the small, combined arms team. By 1968 most Cavalry squadrons and Armored battalions were equipped with M48A3 tanks. They weighed 54.3 tons, sported cast homogeneous steel up to 4.3 inches thick, a 90mm cannon and two machine guns; a .50-Cal. mounted on the turret and a 7.62mm aligned with the main gun in the turret. Three or four men manned each tank; the platoon sergeant led the tank section. The forty men of the platoon were spread evenly among the ten vehicles so that there were three to four men on each ACAV ensuring that every gun was manned.

The vehicles in a cavalry platoon are numbered one through ten. First platoon vehicle numbers carried the prefix one. Thus, my vehicle was 16; my radio call sign was Dapper (the troop's call sign) One-Six. Over time it became conventional to call individuals by their call signs or their nicknames but never by their first name, surname or rank.

---

[1] Donn A. Starry, *Mounted Combat in Vietnam: Department of the Army, Vietnam Series*, Washington, D.C., 1978, p. 38. The author drew heavily on Starry for sections of this writing. Only direct quotations or summaries of specific actions or concepts are footnoted.

I hardly had time to get acquainted with the NCOs and men of 1st Platoon when Squadron Headquarters put A Troop on alert to move out to a village up the beach. C Troop, returning south along the beach, received fire from the fishing village of Binh An. C Troop deployed to extend a line from the beach west around the north side of the village. I rode along with the platoon leader as A Troop rushed north. When the troop reached the southern edge of the village, The CO moved to establish a cordon extending from east to west to a point where we could link up with 1st Cavalry Division infantry battalions flying in from the west. Soon the village of Binh An was surrounded on three sides with its back to the sea.

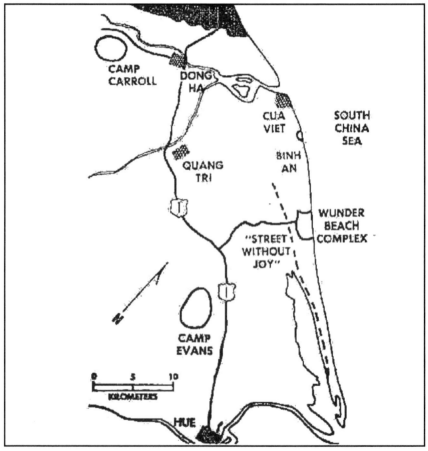

MAP 2: 3rd Squadron 5th Cavalry Area of Operations.
Source: Armor Magazine (July - August 1969)

Battle of Binh An

For the rest of the day the assembled task force pounded Binh An with artillery, air strikes, helicopter rockets, naval guns, our mortars and tank main guns. Just before dark B and C Troops attacked the enemy held village. Ditches and mounds slowed the attacks and exposed the ACAVs, tanks and advancing grunts to heavy RPG and automatic weapons fire. The attack settled down and the Squadron Commander decided to maintain the cordon for the night, continue to hammer the enemy with artillery and naval gunfire and resume the direct attack in the morning.

Shadowing the outgoing platoon leader, I rode in his ACAV and manned the starboard machine gun. For the first time I experienced the din of battle, the snap of passing bullets and their impact as they splintered trees. Beyond that I was a passive observer to all this. Like any ordinary trooper I huddled behind my gun shield and waited for dawn. When it came, it brought a change of plans. Captain McLaughlin, informed that the Squadron Commander was concerned that no cavalry platoon remained at LZ Hard Core to provide security and keep the road between Hard Core and Hai Lang open, directed me to take charge of 1st Platoon, move to Hard Core and take over the Road Runner mission immediately.

The battle of Binh An continued. Before it ended Third Squadron Fifth Cavalry controlled the actions of four battalion size units and coordinated the support of army and marine corps field artillery, aerial rocket artillery, air force fighter-bombers and naval gunfire from the cruiser USS Boston. Over the course of two days the combined effort netted some 275 enemy soldiers of the North Vietnamese Army 814th Battalion killed or captured. General Don Starry later termed it a classic example of the "pile on strategy." [2]

---

[2] Ibid. For a more detailed treatment of the battle, see Ralph B Garretson, Jr., *Armor, July-August 1969*, pp. 25-28.

Chapter Three
Road Runner

We pulled into Hard Core. Without instructions the platoon turned off the road and settled into a line along a bamboo stand on the north side. The men hopped down off their tracks and opened them up. They proceeded to erect sun shields over the tank turrets and the rear openings of the ACAVs using engineer stakes and ponchos. Again, without orders from anyone they set to work cleaning their machine guns and laying out ammunition for the night's mission. Obviously, they had been there before.

    I had barely met Platoon Sergeant (PSG) Fulton before we scrambled out of Wunder Beach to Binh An. In accordance with the original plan to shadow the incumbent platoon leader, I rode along in One-Six. So, I got acquainted with the crew of at least one vehicle. Now, with the whole platoon assembled in one momentarily quiet place and with no immediate distractions, PSG Fulton and I walked down the line and he introduced me to the men of first platoon. I shook hands with all of them focusing on the section leaders and track commanders (TCs). With the time we had I hardly got to know any of them very well except for one. Specialist fourth class (SP4) Terry Reigle, aka "Speedy," was TC of Alpha 16, my command track. He, along with the driver and a gunner, kept the ACAV ship-shape and as time progressed acted as my double when I was off the track or otherwise involved in an action. The rest of the men I got to know better as time and opportunity permitted.

Platoon Sergeant Clarence Fulton

    Having made initial introductions and seeing preparations for the evening's mission underway, I left PSG Fulton with instructions to have the men finish up their preparations and get some rest and something to eat before 1800 hours at which time we would move the platoon across the river and assemble for the Road Run. Meanwhile I had some preparations of my own to make.

    First, I headed to Alpha 10, my mortar track. Staff Sergeant (SSG) Miguel Robles led the mortar team. He was Puerto Rican as it seemed were all the men of his team. Alpha 10 was the unofficial gathering place of the other PRs of the platoon. But my business was not social. I needed to coordinate supporting fire for the mission. Robles and I sat down, and I showed him on my map where I wanted him to set up preplanned illumination and defensive 4.2 mortar fire. I also asked him how many illumination rounds he had and how long they burned. Concluding that forty-five to fifty minutes of light might not be enough if we ran into something big, I decided to coordinate with the other source of light at Hard Core, the artillery.

Picking up my map I headed across the clearing and the road to the church rectory where the resident artillery battery maintained its headquarters. It was the dry season in northern I Corps. The absence of rain and the heavy truck traffic to and from Wunder Beach had ground the packed dirt road to a fine powder of dust up to six inches deep when it was not suspended in the air by the traffic. Come the monsoon the rains turned that dust into a thick pasty mud.

Dodging traffic I made it safely across the road and up the stairs to the second floor of the rectory where the artillery battery maintained its headquarters. I introduced myself and was ignored. The officers, first sergeant and a couple of enlisted men were too busy amusing themselves watching a couple of drunken puppies staggering around the floor after being fed too much beer. Finally pulling themselves away from their entertainment the officers turned their attention to me. I explained who I was, what my mission was and how I needed their support. They became very professional, scoured my map, and told me they could give me nearly continuous light after my 4.2 exhausted its supply of illumination shells. They took the coordinates of my preplanned fires, we exchanged radio frequencies, and I was on my way back to the platoon.

Around 1800 I moved the platoon across the pontoon bridge to the west side of the river and put it in a tight laager, a circular defensive posture not unlike wagon trains in old westerns. I decided to leave the tanks at Hard Core to provide a reaction force if we needed one. The ACAVs were quicker, more agile, quieter and, except for the tank's main guns, could put out a greater volume of fire should we need it. The tanks stayed with 10; PSG Fulton would ride with us.

As dusk turned to full dark, we made our first run from Hard Core to Hai Lang. Road Runs evolved from Thunder Runs commonly used by armored cavalry earlier in the war. Thunder Runs involved moving along roads at night firing random bursts of machine gun fire ahead, alongside and behind the column to interfere with enemy activity whereas Road Runs were more reactive in nature. Our purpose was to draw fire or provoke an ambush. We started out around 22:00 with 13 and 14 in the lead followed by 16,15,11 and 12 at about 30 kpm, spaced far enough apart so that the dust was not in the eyes of the trailing ACAV drivers. Under a clear sky and a light breeze the only sounds were the buzzing bugs and mosquitoes and the distant rumble of the ongoing battle at Binh An. The road to Hai Lang ran straight with a couple of jogs left or right. With rice paddies and drainage ditches on either side we enjoyed clear fields of fire except where local farming villages crowded in. We made the first run and returned to the assembly point where we laggard up until the next run. Piece of cake.

About an hour later we did it again. Halfway to Hai Lang where the road passed a village to our right and took a little jog to the left, 11 came up on the platoon net. "One-Six this is One-One, over?" "One-Six, Go." "One-One, I can't see One-Two behind me, over?" I called a halt and an about face and started back with guns blazing. We soon came upon 12 in the middle of the road leaning down to its right. Quickly the five ACAVs put a tight perimeter around 12 and continued firing and popping hand-held flares in every direction. PSG Fulton dismounted 11 on which he had been riding and dashed to 12 to check things out. Meanwhile I ordered each ACAV to dismount two men and one machine gun and fill in the spaces between the ACAVs making up the perimeter. I also called 10 and told him to put up some light as hand-held flares did not put out that much or last especially long.

PSG Fulton suddenly appeared at my side to tell me everyone on 12 was alive but needed a Medevac. "I don't know how to do that," I replied. "You take care of it, and I'll work on the perimeter." We split up to take care of our respective tasks. The platoon continued firing in every direction. No one could tell if we were receiving fire, so I called a cease fire. As I moved among the tracks checking on what if any fire they had received and from what direction it was coming, I heard small arms shots from the perimeter facing the village. Dashing in that direction my leg went out from under me and I went down. Back on my feet I came to the section receiving fire and ordered them to cease fire while we determined what we were facing. It appeared that we were taking occasional sniper fire from the direction of the village. I got things settled down and told the men to keep their counter fire to a minimum, shooting only when the sniper revealed himself by his muzzle flash and then only in the direction of fire.

SSG Robles had done a good job keeping us lit up while all this was going on, but he was running out of illumination rounds. I called the artillery. "This is Dapper One-Six Fire mission, over?" Pause. Silence. "Dapper One-Six Fire...." "WHO IS THIS? What the fuck are you doing on my firing frequency? Get the fuck off!" Again, silence. Next thing I heard was, "Dapper One-Six this is Mustang Two (squadron Intelligence officer), sounds like you've got a little situation there." I quickly explained. Told to wait, I did. Shortly the artillery came online, gave me a new frequency, and we renewed our conversation. All of this was very unorthodox and a clear violation of radio security. But we got the job done, and soon I had a steady stream of light if we needed it.

Meanwhile, under PSG Fulton's guidance we got the crew of 12 out via dust off. All four men would survive. Some would come back. I could not remember one of their names.

Ambushed ACAV

Settling down for the night, I maintained the perimeter in place and put the men on fifty percent watch. PSG Fulton and I stayed up making sure those on watch stayed awake and alert. Fulton accomplished this by patrolling the line and firing off occasional rounds from an M79 grenade launcher. Around 04:00 I called the artillery and told them they could turn out the light.

Morning came and with it a crowd of visitors. First to arrive were a company of South Vietnamese soldiers from Hai Lang; not ARVN but Regional Forces/Popular Forces affectionately known as RUFF/PUFF. Equivalent to our National Guard, they searched the area, especially the village, and the roadsides.

Next came a squadron maintenance vehicle accompanied by two of my tanks. The maintenance vehicle, an M88 VTR (Vehicle Tank Recovery), was a rolling armored machine shop and tow truck. The mechanics quickly took charge of 12, hoisted it on to a heavy truck, and took it back to Wunder Beach. While 12 was in the air we got a good look at the damage and the mine crater. From the crater we decided that 12 had hit a command detonated mine; probably a large artillery round buried in the road set off by an electronic detonator off to the side of the road. The mine blew a hole clear through the right front corner of 12's armored hull, engine compartment and gear box. It was a total loss. Following a closer examination of the drainage ditch by the road we found several post card size placards enjoining Black American soldiers from serving the white capitalists and urging them to join the National Liberation Front. (See Appendix I)

Our final visitor of the day was Mustang Six, 3/5 Cavalry's squadron CO. He flew in in his command helicopter, asked for a briefing, and walked around the area. After I briefed him, he took PSG Fulton aside, no doubt to ask him how I did. Returning to me, he shook my hand and said, "Good job," and was gone. Years later at a Squadron Reunion, I introduced myself and recounted the Incident. "That was you?" he said. "You don't know how lucky you were. If that had been the only incident at the time, you'd of had all the colonels and generals in I Corps stacked up overhead demanding your report and offering their guidance."

Later that afternoon PSG Fulton and I gathered up the platoon and returned to Hard Core. I went on to Wunder Beach where the squadron surgeon tended to the minor flesh wound in my leg while I sipped the bourbon-on-the-rocks he prepared for me.

I had been a platoon leader for exactly twenty-four hours.

Chapter Four
Life on the Street

Things settled down to a routine after that. A Troop resumed its part in the Squadron's mission. We continued to Road Run between Hard Core and Hai Lang, conduct search and control operations along The Street, the dunes and coast, and support Rome Plow operations at the southern end of the AO near Hue on a rotating basis with B and C Troops. Gradually, I came to know the men of 1st Platoon and appreciate them. About half of them were draftees and proud that they were cavalry men. Those who were not draftees, even those who were classified infantry, MOS 11B, did not consider themselves Grunts, the classic appellation for the infantry. Almost to a man, they got along with one another. I detected no sign of racial animosity among them as I had in the Sixth Cavalry. They worked well together and backed one another up.

They called PSG Fulton "The Shadow." He was soft spoken and knew something about each man. Slow to anger, he moved quietly among the men encouraging and guiding them rather than ordering them about. I experienced The Shadow's technique the first time I bought beer and soft drinks for the platoon. Squadron policy permitted each man two beers daily on evenings when they were not in the field or going out on ambush after dark. Fulton sat down next to me afterward and quietly thanked me for the purchase and then said, "You ought not make that a habit One-Six. The guys could come to expect it and get too familiar with you. Besides," he added, "you need to be savin' your money for when you get home and marry that Miss Doyle." I never did find out how he learned Jo's name.

Meanwhile, we had to deal with a new squadron commander. On July 2, 1968, Lieutenant Colonel Hugh Bartley turned over command of Third Squadron Fifth Cavalry to Lieutenant Colonel Angelo Grills. Where COL Bartley was an earthy, approachable squadron commander, Grills proved himself something of a self-important prig. As soon as he took command, he ordered that we could no longer buy ice from the locals. There was an ice factory in Hai Lang where civilian Vietnamese bought ice and sold it to us outside of Hard Core. A five-dollar chunk fit perfectly in the mermite coolers every track had. It lasted about a day and kept beer and soda tolerably cool. During his pre-command orientation, Grills probably heard that the VC sometimes booby-trapped ice by freezing grenades with their pins pulled inside blocks of ice. When the ice melted, boom! Hence, we drank warm beer or Coke. Likewise, he forbade the troops from sending their fatigues out to be washed at local laundries. I never did learn the rationale behind that, but soon we were all doing our own. This was even more galling when we learned that Grills and the headquarters staff were getting their own laundry done locally.

Search and control operations involved crisscrossing the dunes randomly and cordoning fishing villages on the coast, farming villages on The Street and checking graveyards in the dunes for rice and arms caches. During the day we surrounded a village or area of interest, dismounted foot patrols who entered local hooches looking for military-age men, checking their papers and detaining those without them. We also probed hooch floors and in and around village common areas where freshly disturbed earth suggested a recent burial. Occasionally we would find rice in excess to a village's needs. This was deemed VC and evacuated. We also found weapons and equipment, usually AK47s, radios and, occasionally, a random M16.

Working the villages and dunes was hot work. When the temperature approached 120 degrees Mac would suspend activity and pull the troop off to the beach or one of the larger intermittent ponds in the dunes where we laggard and went swimming. We spent the rest of the day and night at these locations putting out ambushes and listening posts. The times we spent laggard on the beach or in the dunes did wonders for morale. Because of the open terrain, it was possible to keep only one man on watch per track. PSG Fulton insisted that I not share watch; he wanted me wide awake all day. I took to sleeping on a stretcher across the rear ramp of A16 during those occasions. It also served as my "office" where my NCOs and I would meet to review the events of the day and discuss any lessons learned to be passed to the troopers.

On these occasions, Top would come out in late afternoon bringing the mail, supplies and a section of the mess team to provide a hot meal. He also returned men from sick call, R&R and those coming off duties such as KP. In the morning he reversed the process. Following a hot breakfast, he rounded up men scheduled for KP, R&R and those wanting to go on sick call, packed up the mess team and headed back to Wunder Beach. Top hated these trips into the field; Indian Country as he termed it. He was a veteran of the Korean War and knew the risks small units moving in unsecure territory faced. Nevertheless, of course, he did it, and in doing so he kept his finger on the pulse of the troop as no officer could.

By this time, I had a new driver for A16. My original driver left at the end of his tour. Red Pennington, former driver of A12, the ACAV blown up on my first day as Platoon Leader, just returned from his injuries, filled right in, and proved to be an excellent driver.

During my first month as platoon leader, I went native. Not wanting to stand out conspicuously from the rest of the men, I dressed casually forgoing patches and insignia of rank. Because of the heat and humidity, I stopped wearing underwear and socks, and took on a scruffy appearance. I also started growing a mustache as part of my cavalry demeanor.

Our time patrolling The Street, dunes and seaside sounds almost idyllic. It was not. We found rice and weapons during the daily patrols. It was during our nighttime efforts that we killed, wounded, or captured the VC/NVA and disrupted their activities. We did this by ambushing them as they moved across the dunes or met in villages to plan future operations. It was hairy work. Cavalry men were not too keen on dismounting their tracks at night and going after the bad guys on foot or laying in ambush suffering fly and mosquito attacks in silence awaiting the chance that some careless VC would walk into their killing zone. My ranger training proved useful in this regard as we sent out ambushes nightly. I checked out each ambush patrol to ensure they did not carry anything that could alert VC/NVA to their presence like personal radios, food and cigarettes or bug repellent. Instead, I had them roll in dirt and dust to mask their body odor to bugs. These measures worked to a point, but, in the absence of frequent contact with the enemy, it proved difficult to break personal habits.

We made several innovations to multiply our advantages. Once while searching a village on The Street, Second Platoon left a four man stay-behind team in a hooch. Later that night a couple of VC suspects came into the hooch. Quickly subdued, the VC were captured and extracted by a team waiting outside the village. Local authorities identified them as VC, but because they had papers released them. We nicknamed the older of the two "Luc the Gook" and set him free. We picked him up again a few days later as he was crossing the dunes moving inland. Again, local authorities released him. For his troubles we gave Luc a couple of C-ration boxes and dropped him off at the edge of town.

A couple of weeks later we pulled off one of our most audacious night operations. CPT Mac conceived a night cordon and search of a large fishing village on the edge of the dunes. With LTC Grills' approval, Mac took 1st and 2nd Platoons, a platoon of D Troop, 1/9 Cavalry attached from the 1st Cavalry Division and our 3rd Platoon's tank section on a sweeping march around the village. They certainly heard us but could not see us in the dark. Once we completed the encirclement, Mac had the ACAVs and tanks face inward and turn on their lights. The tanks' Xenon searchlights bathed the village in bright light. Third Platoon remained outside the cordon to intercept any villagers attempting to evade capture.

Assisted by local police equipped with bull horns we ordered the villagers out of their hooches and herded them into two groups: old men, women and children and military age men. Then grunts from D/1/9 and cavalry men moved into the former group looking for military age men hiding among the women and old men. Immediately a hue and cry went up from the women. Crying and howling they clung to those men and teenage boys trying to evade our troops. Just as suddenly another voice arose quickly silencing the others. It was Luc. Pointing to CPT Mac he assured the villagers that we were okay and that they should cooperate with us. After that we were able to finish searching the village and detaining men without papers or identified by police as VC suspects. We liberated several hundred pounds of VC rice but no weapons from the village that night. We never learned whether any of the detainees turned out to be VC, but Luc showed up a few days later. He never failed to wave and flash a smile which we always returned. As far as I know he was still there when 3/5 Cavalry left Wunder Beach at the end of October.

Patrolling The Street itself presented different challenges. South of where Route 602 (Sky King Highway) intersected The Street stood several villages a few kilometers apart. A church or temple anchored each village of hooches. Like every village both men and women worked in the rice paddies from dawn to dusk. Only the elderly, children and women with infants remained in the village during daylight hours. This made it difficult to get to the military age males. This necessitated the use of more ambushes and night patrols to catch those Vietnamese out of their villages after dark. In the dunes east of QL555 we set ambushes on known footpaths between The Street and villages on the coast. West of The Street few such paths existed; canals and waterways feeding the rice paddies represented the preferred mode of travel absent finished roads. We set drop-off ambushes at crossing points of the smaller canals. Where the presence of makeshift kayaks or larger flat-bottomed skiffs suggested larger, frequently used crossing points, we set mounted ambushes by dropping off an ACAV above or below stream of the crossing site, these ambushes rarely proved productive and once almost disastrous. On that occasion I accompanied a mounted ambush of two ACAVs from my scout section led by Staff Sergeant M. L Faltus. Known as "Pappy" to all, Faltus, like SSG Richard Block of 2nd platoon, was an original. Tall, lean, and scruffy, Pappy knew his job and did it well. I have a fond memory of him bartering a can of beer for a sun umbrella from an elderly Vietnamese couple we encountered on a particularly hot day of patrolling.

On the night of the ambush in question, we set up above and below the target area so we could see any traffic approaching from either direction. As usual, especially near water bodies, insects swarmed us. Not risking giving our position away by using army issued insecticide, we suffered in silence. Sometime after midnight we heard the unmistakable buzz of a helicopter approaching from the south. We could see and hear machine gun fire spewing into the banks of the canal. It did not take any time at all to figure out that, even though we had registered our ambush position, someone was conducting reconnaissance by fire. I broke radio silence and called Mac appraising him of our situation. He checked with squadron and brigade headquarters and assured me that our position was registered. But he cautioned that because we were near the southern boundary of the AO, adjacent units may not have been notified. Worse still the helicopter may have strayed off its course concentrating on its mission. I had no alternative but to cancel the ambush. We turned on our lights, popped some hand flares, got everyone inside the ACAVs and buttoned up. The helicopter passed over us, paused firing, and continued its way. No harm, no foul, but we never did another mounted waterside ambush again.

There is a saying that the difference between the Army and the Boy Scouts is that the Boy Scouts have adult leadership. Combat breeds a certain cynicism and dark humor. During breaks between combat or when constant patrolling in the same area without contact with the enemy, daily life becomes routine. At times like these soldiers look for ways to entertain themselves either individually through practical jokes or collectively by conducting bizarre activities.

South of the inhabited part of The Street lay several abandoned villages marked only by their ruined churches or temples. Between late June and early August, we explored the remains of the villages as part of our routine assignments. One of the churches, dubbed the church with one steeple, still had its bell. We had to have it. It would be perfect for our mess hall. The nearby church with two steeples did not have a bell, and the temple had a huge gong that was too big for our purpose. Besides, the temple lay just outside of the squadron AO. We platoon leaders with CPT Mac's active support turned our attention to the church with one steeple.

Everyone had an idea of how to separate the bell from the steeple without damaging either. The yoke of the bell was set into the steeple's masonry. We tried loosening the masonry that held the yoke fast. When that did not work, we tried pulling it down with tow cables linked together and pulled by a tank. When neither approach succeeded, we turned to the army's standard technique for breaking things – C4 plastic explosive. Carefully measuring the size of the yoke and drilling out more masonry we packed the holes with C4 and hooked up detonators on either side of the bell. The idea was to set the detonators to go off simultaneously assuring that the bell came straight down. We even set a pile of brush in the atrium to cushion the bell's fall.

With everything ready we backed off. Troopers of all ranks bet on the outcome. The explosion kicked up a huge cloud of dust and debris. Instinctively I knew we had used too much explosive. As the dust cleared, we found that we had created a church with no steeple. Poking through the rubble it also became clear that we had also shattered the bell. Wanton war damage? We did not think so at the time. Later, I decided that blowing up that church was not one of my prouder moments. We immediately set about to take another look at the temple. Before we could do that, we rotated missions with B and C Troops.

The Rome Plow operation at the southern end of the Squadron's AO involved providing round the clock security to a team of behemoth armored bulldozers that cleared swaths of forests and jungle near tactically important areas. In this instance the forested area was known to have provided cover and concealment to NVA troops that took over Hue during the Tet Offensive earlier in 1968. We patrolled the perimeters of the plow's path as they uprooted trees and undergrowth. They attracted snipers determined to stop or slow their efforts to deny the enemy sanctuary.

The mission had its obvious challenges as well as some challenges unique to armored track vehicles. The high water table combined with the shifting sand of the dunes created pools of quicksand that our tanks and ACAVs encountered frequently. Vehicle recovery operations proved more complicated than those we faced during training at Fort Knox. For one thing nobody was sniping at us while we struggled to free a mired ACAV. The loose and shifting sand provided an additional hazard, especially to tanks; thrown tracks. Again, the school solution did not work so well when a tank threw is track to the inside of its road wheels and under the tank's belly. Once, when faced with such a dilemma, we ended up deploying the platoon around the stranded tank while we worked on it through the night. The lights necessary to complete the recovery attracted more than one sniper. PSG Fulton resorted to his usual method of keeping the platoon awake and alert through the night by popping off M79 rounds occasionally. Amazingly, no one was hit by the snipers, and by morning we had the tank operational again. Then it was back to Wunder Beach where Colonel Grills waited to present us with a new challenge.

Chapter Five
One Too Many Rivers

On our way back to Wunder Beach we took a swing through some of the villages on The Street. Just at dusk, 2nd Platoon that was in the lead unexpectedly (given the racket the tanks were making) flushed a small patrol of Gooks. Without waiting for instructions, I raced 1st Platoon ahead and turned inward to block the Gooks. Third Platoon closed the cordon, and we all began shooting inward. We were sure we had them as several tracks reported receiving fire from inside the cordoned area. It could be, on the other hand, that, as was often the case, the fire was coming from our own guns on the opposite side of the cordon. Nevertheless, we blazed away.

Suddenly, a flash and explosion lit up my machine gun on the port side of A16.

I felt a burning sensation in my right arm. My immediate thought was that a bullet had hit the gun shield and ricocheted in to the gun itself. Later we figured out that the machine gun double-fed one round on top of another, causing the second to explode in the receiver instead of the chamber. The exploding round peppered my arm with brass casing and gun powder without breaking skin. Doc slathered my arm with salve and wrapped it with a bandage. That was that.

Meanwhile, Mac called a cease fire and ordered each platoon to dismount scouts to check the area. Naturally, no one was particularly anxious to thoroughly check out the cordoned area as it was now completely dark. Mac decided to maintain the cordon through the night and do a more complete search at dawn.

We did exactly that and found some bloody clothes and abandoned packs. Mac concluded that some bad guys had been there but got away in the confusion and dark. Squadron was badgering Mac to get back to Headquarters on the double to prepare for the new mission set to begin the following day.

Rumors had begun circulating that 3/5 Cavalry would be returning south once the monsoon began in the northern part of the country. At the same time American units were expected to conduct more operations with ARVN units. Colonel Grills planned to kill two birds with one stone by conducting a river crossing with South Vietnamese Army units. The scenario he painted involved A Troop making a hasty river crossing aimed at catching NVA/VC in between. The ARVN would set up a blocking force into which we would drive the bad guys. Lost in the briefing, at least to us platoon leaders, was the fact that this was a training exercise designed to prepare us for the rumored move back to the wetter south.

Things started out well enough the next morning as we moved out to our objective. First Platoon took the lead with 2nd and 3rd platoons following. Mac rode between me and 2nd platoon. We headed almost due south for about seven kilometers through paddies and across irrigation canals. We must have won many hearts and minds as we churned our way through those paddies. Finally, we halted and made the necessary preparations to cross the river before taking up the blocking position.

M113 armored personnel carriers were designed to "swim", ford streams and rivers under their own power carrying an infantry squad and its equipment. They had rubber skirts that partially covered their tracks to provide a little buoyancy and a front mounted wooden trim-vane to prevent displaced water from flooding the driver's hatch and intake for the air-cooled engine. As modified with shields and three machine guns, the ACAV could perform the same function; except when heavy use damaged the skirts and trim vane. Even then a skilled driver could manage an ACAV across a water body.

A Troop approached the west bank of the O Giang River. First Platoon would cross upstream and second downstream. Mac held third platoon in reserve. All the tanks and mortar sections took up positions overlooking the far bank. Since this was a hasty river crossing, we made no provisions for preparatory or covering fire.

In we went. With one of my scouts in the lead and A16 following, things went badly from the start. The lead vehicle got twisted in the currant and foundered almost immediately. Red got A16 around the sinking scout and kept going. Behind us A15 was in trouble. The TC, SGT Howie Pitts, panicked. He and the others on board started shifting their weight causing the track to lurch side to side. "One-Six this is One-Five, over." Pitts called, fear echoing in his voice. "This is One-Five," he hollered. "Ahm sinkin, Ahm sinkin, Ahm sinkin an I caint swim!" One of my other scouts was also in trouble. A13 hit an uneven spot in the riverbed. It threw him off course and spun him around. His driver over compensated and spun back around causing water to slosh into the cargo hold. Down he went. I had lost three of my six ACAVS.

I and one other had made it across, the remaining track turned back. I ordered that track back to the far side, and, since we had been told there were VC in the area, popped a few 40mm grenades off as a precaution. As we pulled back to return to the river, I noticed a civilian on the ground. A dog was pulling or chewing on its ankle. Had I done that? I did not give it a second thought as we put A16 back in the water and headed back.

Great River Crossing

LONG AGO AND FAR AWAY • 33

GIs can find humor in just about anything. Moving back across the river I saw Don Sizemore do a cannon ball off his track oblivious to the situation. He and his crew were using the time to cool off in the river. Platoon Sergeant Fulton paddled up to them in a commandeered dugout to check things out and moved on to the other sunk ACAVs. They were not down so deep. Like Sizemore their crews sat atop the ACAVs just awash in the river clinging to the radio antennas for safety.

As we emerged on the friendly side of the river, I saw MAJ Nick Kraciew, the new Squadron Operations Officer overseeing the recovery of one of my three drowned vehicles. I remembered him from West Point. He waved, gave me a sardonic smile and said, "All in a day's work, lieutenant, all in a day's work."

Back at Wunder Beach before dark, we began the cleanup. One of my TCs had the presence of mind to kill his engine before it sucked water into it. That one could be repaired quickly; the other two would need new engines. Everybody cleaned out their water-logged gear. Meanwhile, Mac and we platoon leaders tried to figure out what had happened. In addition to my three, second platoon lost two ACAVs. Third platoon was spared by the fact that it was not in the first wave of the crossing, and of course, there never was a second wave. But if this was to be a portent of things to come as we returned south, we all had a stake in the outcome.

Everyone had an opinion. The river was faster and deeper than we had been told or expected. Every vehicle that sank was missing one or both skirts and lacked a trim vane. The drivers lacked enough or had not any training. In the final analysis, though, at least in the opinion of Colonel Grills, the problem was that the ACAVs were too heavy. The solution, therefore, was to off load a layer of ammunition. The troopers and NCOs were livid. The extra layer of ammunition was their security blanket. They had been known to burn through a layer in less than a day of hard fighting. It was not always possible to resupply in a day. Nevertheless, word went out to the line troops to accomplish the task at once. B and C Troops complied; Mac decided to sleep on it. We turned in for the night.

Oh, one more thing. SGT Pitts' ACAV did sink, but he did not. Like any other enterprising enlisted man Pitts took advantage of the opportunity to cool off in the river and take a bath. He just did not swim.

Chapter Six
Van Phong

In the morning, Top had a hot breakfast ready for us, a rare luxury. Captain Mac told us platoon leaders to make sure everyone ate first and then clean up themselves and their tracks. Then he disappeared in the direction of Squadron HQ. He returned about an hour later and called us together again along with Top and the platoon sergeants. To our relief and disbelief, he told us he had negotiated a twenty-four-hour stand down with Colonel Grills. This was to be a complete stand down for the line platoons. The only work we were to do was complete first echelon maintenance on the tracks, rearm and resupply. Headquarters platoon would remain open for business; the mess section was to prepare a cold cut lunch and hot dinner for the whole troop, the supply and maintenance sections and the armorer would remain available to assist the platoons with any repair, supply or weapons needs. After lunch everyone was ordered to take the afternoon off, Top would organize a trip to the beach for those who wanted a swim. After dinner everyone had the night off except for the usual interior guard in the motor pool and Troop HQ.

PSG Fulton and I went about the business of informing the platoon. I emphasized that everyone, including Fulton, take the afternoon to rest, write letters home, go to the beach or whatever. I intended to do the same.

After lunch I showered and put on fresh fatigues and clean socks. In no time at all I was hot and sweating. I went back to A16 and found it was crowded with Red, Speedy and a couple of visitors. They offered to move, but I wanted someplace more private to write some letters and make a tape to send to Jo. Wandering down the little stream behind us I came upon an abandoned bunker I had not seen previously. It was a small two- or three-man sandbag bunker with a sheet metal roof covered with more sandbags no doubt abandoned when the prime tenants expanded the base perimeter. I crawled inside. It was damp but cool. A sea breeze was blowing in from the Tonkin Gulf. From the gun slots I could see the Gulf and some scrub pines and grass swaying in the wind. Perfect. I settled down to do my letters and promptly dozed off.

I awoke with a start. Someone was calling my name. Squirming out of the bunker I ran toward the caller. It was Pappy. Squadron had alerted us; we were to be ready to move out in thirty minutes. I hotfooted it over to the platoon; it was gone. I found it already lining up with the rest of the troop in the motor pool. I headed toward A16 where PSG Fulton was waiting. He gave me a quick sitrep (Situation Report) to bring me up to date. I climbed aboard A16, tied into the platoon net, and got a status report from all my tracks. Switching to the troop net I reported us ready.

On Mac's order A Troop moved out in column. Speedy waved his machete as we picked up the pace. Suddenly SGT Don Sizemore appeared running alongside. "Take me with you, LT," he yelled, "First Sergeant fucks with us when you leave us behind." Without giving it much thought I pulled him aboard and sat him behind the starboard machine gun. "Doc" our medic was between us.

A Troop pulled out of the main gate and headed northwest. In the distance we could see smoke and helicopters circling. CPT Mac came up on the net and briefed us platoon leaders on the situation:

A company of First Battalion, Eighth Cavalry, First Cavalry Division to which 3/5 Cavalry was under OPCON (Operational Control) had been operating for the last three weeks north of The Street to flush out local VC and look for weapons and rice caches. This morning, near the village of Van Phong, they detained two suspected VC and called for a helicopter to extract them. As the helicopter came in, it and the party holding the suspects received heavy fire. The CO of 1/8 Cavalry sent in more troops and soon the whole battalion was involved. The amount of enemy fire convinced the commander of 1/8 that he was dealing with more than local VC. He called for more support, and soon had ARA helicopter gunships and A Troop, 3/5 Cavalry on the way. C Troop was coming down from the north to join us.[3]

---

[3] Much of what follows is supported by 1/8 Cavalry Battalion's daily staff journal for the month of August 1968, a copy is in the author's possession. See especially entries for 20 and 21 August.

As we arrived at the vicinity of Van Phong, Mac had the column of 2nd and 1st platoons peel off to the left and 3rd platoon to the right. Second platoon made contact with the infantry who began to intersperse themselves between our tracks while third platoon tied in with C Troop when it arrived on the battlefield. Once those maneuvers were accomplished, he had the troop come on-line and advance toward the woodline where the enemy fire was coming from. The aim was to squeeze the enemy into a more confined area and pile on with concentrated ground artillery fire as we did at Binh An.

The enemy fire became more intense. Brigade put control of the battle under 1/8 Cavalry whose CO ordered the advance to halt and dig in. We adjusted our positions by moving through the dry paddies and up to the paddy dikes that gave the infantry some cover. My people hunkered down behind their machine gun shields. Most of the enemy fire was going into the paddy dikes and over the tracks. Probably, I theorized later, because we rode on top of our tracks causing the enemy to aim high. This was precisely why 18th and 19th century infantry wore tall shakoes.

We were less than 200 meters from the woodline where the most intense fire was coming from. Captain Mac ordered us to prepare for "danger close," meaning that we would be within the bursting radius of the incoming artillery rounds. I spread the word to my tracks and the infantry between them. "Shot, over," Mac called; the artillery was on the way.

I remember hearing, more sensing, the first round pass over us. The next thing I remembered was being sprawled on the deck of A16 pawing around looking for my glasses. They always seemed to come off when we hit shit. Speedy later said that he pushed me. At the same time, I was yelling, "CEASE FIRE, CHECK FIRE, JESUS FUCKING CHRIST, CEASE FIRE" on the radio. I found my glasses, put them on and stood up to see what happened. Sizemore was on his back, hanging on to his machine gun unnaturally with one hand. He was beginning to gurgle. Doc and Speedy were working on him. My first conscious thought was, "I'm glad I have my rain suit on; otherwise, I'd have this mud and gore (Sizemore) all over my fresh fatigues." I told Speedy to take charge of A16 and hopped off to check the rest of the platoon. I ran up and down the line checking each track and the infantry men between them. We had eight men down: Sizemore and seven grunts. I called for a dust off and continued checking with the line yelling instructions to firm it up and prepare for a counterattack. No doubt the enemy had seen what happened and could take advantage of the situation. With darkness increasing I kept working my section of the line finally returning to A16 around 20:00. As I reached A16, I stumbled and fell over a body in the mud. "Here's another one," I called out to no one in particular. An NCO, I think he was an E6 came to my assistance with a flashlight. I wiped the mud from the downed man's face; it was Fulton. He must have come up to the left-rear of 16 to coordinate with me when the long round hit, killing him instantly.

I called Speedy to kick down a stretcher and poncho. The NCO and I along with a couple of grunts got Fulton on the stretcher and covered him with the poncho. I grabbed the left-front handle to carry him to a waiting dust off and felt a hand on my shoulder. "Steady lieutenant," a voice said, "we're going to need you tonight." "This is my Platoon Sergeant," I muttered. "I'm going to get him on his way." We carried him to the helicopter and handed him up to the medics.

The chopper took off. I waved and turned back to the business at hand.

Back on A16 I did a quick assessment of our situation. Including the Infantry, we had three killed (Sizemore died on the way to the hospital.) and seven wounded; all evacuated. All my tracks were up and running. We had enough ammunition. I had each track give extra M16 ammunition to the grunts between their tracks. Our position was firm. The infantry remained dug in behind the paddy dikes that provided some cover for the tracks. I appointed Staff Sergeant Philips, tank section leader acting platoon sergeant, briefed him, and headed off down the line toward A66 to brief CPT Mac and get his instructions.

I updated Mac on our situation giving him a firm accounting of our dead and wounded, including Fulton's and Sizemore's service numbers. I also reported on our fuel and ammunition status and the platoon's morale which, in my estimation, was good. He concurred with my appointment of SSG Philips as acting platoon sergeant. Mac brought me up to date on the other platoons that had some casualties but remained effective. The plan for the night was to remain in place, keep the cordon tight, and thwart any enemy attempts to break out. He added that we would get air strikes, more artillery and ARA as soon as it became light enough to see the target area. I headed back to 1st Platoon and passed the word that we would maintain a 50 percent alert level and go to 100 percent half an hour before first light.

At some point during the night, I had a dissociative experience. From the time I stumbled on Fulton's body until I returned from my meeting with Mac,

I observed myself and my actions from an elevated position slightly over my shoulder. It was like I was watching events unfold but not having a role in them. Finally, back on A16, having briefed the platoon and set the watch, things settled down and I returned to my body. Now I had time to reflect. How had I done? Had I managed my portion of the battle, right? How had the platoon done? Usually, Fulton and I would talk over the events of the day over a warm beer once we had closed in for the night. Now Fulton was gone. Had I contributed to his death? And what about Sizemore? He should have remained behind at Wunder Beach. Squadron policy dictated that the TC and driver of a downed track remain with it to assist in its repair. I did not sleep at all that night. I knew these events would haunt me for a long time. And they did.

Chapter Seven
Bac Ta

Morning twilight began about an hour before dawn. Sitreps began coming in from the rest of the platoon. Everyone was up and ready. Our first order from Mac was to back up a couple hundred yards from our present positions and place orange day-glow panels on the backs of our tracks. Pulling back took us right past the crater that marked the impact of the long round that killed Fulton, Sizemore, the 1/8 Infantry grunt and wounded seven others. I had not seen it before; rather I had experienced it. Now, with time to reflect, I could see Sizemore gagging on his own blood struggling to survive. I could see myself wiping the mud from Fulton's lifeless face. Looking at the crater filled with muddy water, I felt sick to my stomach. Hard to imagine that it happened less than a day ago. Little passed between Red, Speedy and me or for that matter between the rest of the platoon and me while we waited for the morning's events to unfold. Like every other member of the platoon, I was exhausted and numb.

Most mornings at that time of year in Northern I Corps the rising sun stimulated wispy trails of smoke like transpiration skyward from the trees. As the sun rose higher so did the heat and humidity. Soon we could see each other's tracks and the woodline that we had been unable to penetrate the evening before. The men were going about their usual morning routines. They peed and pooped behind their tracks, wolfed down a breakfast of cold Cs and remounted their tracks.

Suddenly, with little warning, a pair of Air Force "thuds" screeched from east to west over our heads unloading snake and nape into the tree line. The trees erupted in blossoms of flame accompanied by the crump of explosions and oily black smoke. Speedy and I exchanged approving glances while guys on the other tracks cheered and called for more. Obligingly the Thuds pivoted around and came back for another pass. This time they preceded their bomb run with long bursts of 20mm machine gun fire that sounded like a heard of wild animals stampeding through the otherwise still forest. After delivering another load of bombs and napalm they were gone, followed by 1st Cav helicopter gunships firing ARA and 7.62 machine guns. They were done as quickly as the ground support fighter jets, but, unlike the Air Force, they loitered in case they were needed while the grunts moved into the impact area to assess the damage done to the enemy. There were none to be found.

One could almost hear the airways buzzing between the cavalry and infantry headquarters as they deliberated what to do next. Finally, the grunts were ordered to thoroughly search the area in and around Van Phong while A Troop swept south along The Street as far as LZ Hard Core probing each village and hamlet to flush out any of the enemy who may have escaped the night before. C Troop returned to its mission further north near Quang Tri.

We started out around noon. Second Platoon led with two columns abreast, scouts leading followed by infantry, tanks, and their mortar track. My platoon followed in the same formation, while third platoon trailed in reserve. Almost immediately, one of Second Platoon's scouts came upon an abandoned hooch that the VC or NVA had used recently as a training site. The walls of the hooch were covered with charcoal drawings of maps of the surrounding area. Most prominent among the drawings were sketches showing helicopters in the air and machine guns shooting at them in high and low crossfire. This is exactly what had happened the day before drawing 1/8 Infantry into the fight that resulted in Fulton's and Sizemore's deaths. As word spread among the troop, the mission suddenly took on new meaning.

A Troop continued to probe south along The Street. The day was hot and sticky. Nobody minded much as it seemed we had picked up the enemy's trail. Around 1600 hours Second Platoon took small arms fire from a cop of trees perhaps 100 meters to its right. Swinging to its right Block's platoon deliberately assaulted the position. With three ACAVs abreast and infantry between and behind the tracks they closed on the enemy who fled to the west toward an apparently abandoned hamlet called Bac Ta. Soon the whole Troop was in pursuit. I was elated and I could sense that the whole platoon was too. We were sure we had caught up with the NVA/VC unit that was responsible for Fulton's death. We could taste blood.

First, we had to run them to ground. That proved harder than expected. We did not want the enemy to slip away in the dark as they had the night before. It was already dusk. More helicopter gunships, artillery and "Puff the Magic Dragon" came to our assistance. Puff was a C-130 modified to carry machine guns fired through ports on its side. With an apparent endless supply of ammunition, Puff pinned the enemy in place and loitered to keep it from moving until dawn.

Meanwhile, we had some logistical chores to accomplish. After the dash from Wunder Beach and two days of fighting we were running low on fuel and ammunition. Larry Pate, the troop XO, led a resupply convoy made up of mechanics, and other headquarters platoon personnel including First Sergeant Paige, to a site behind our position. Just the act of getting trucks carrying fuel, M-88 tank recovery vehicles and random M-113s through the dunes and scrub pines in the dark took guts. The next step proved just as hairy. Pate, 1st SGT Paige and their ad hoc team spent the rest of the night pulling platoon ACAVs in ones and twos off the line and back to the improvised resupply point in blackout conditions where they were topped off with fuel and ammunition. The mechanics also checked each track while the crews received hot coffee and pastry. By the end of the night some twenty-five or so tracks and their crews had been serviced.

As soon as it got light enough to see, A Troop moved in for the kill. We swept online with all guns blazing and quickly closed on a wide canal that ran northwest to southeast parallel to The Street from Quang Tri to Hard Core. Coming about the troop returned to its starting point methodically firing at anything that could harbor the enemy. Reinforced bunkers dotted Bac Ta providing cover to the enemy. We used our tanks to blast the bunkers and ride over and crush them. At one point, A16 got stuck going over a bunker. I had to dismount and direct the platoon on foot while Speedy freed it. Dismounting under fire was a scary proposition. Most cavalrymen drew a false sense of security from the gun shields of their ACAVs to the point that some even set aside their flak jackets during firefights. Once A16 was operational again I remounted, shaken but none the worse for the scare. Then we came about again and re swept the ground already covered. It was exhilarating! Never had I felt so good about killing Gooks.

Attack at Bac Ta

By 0900 hours it was over. Once we were confident that there was no fire coming from the enemy we dismounted and scoured the battlefield on foot. We counted thirty-five dead, took captive two wounded NVA and collected twenty-two weapons, including light machine guns, mortars and RPG launchers and rockets. A search of the bodies revealed useful information. From the contents of their letters. we learned that they were indeed NVA. Most wore fresh uniforms and carried extra, clean uniforms in their packs; some packs contained NVA battle flags. This, along with letters not yet sent home suggested that they had recently crossed the DMZ into South Vietnam. Their morale was high, and they were spoiling for a fight. They were from the heavy weapons company of the K8 Battalion, NVA.

Captured enemy weapons

During the search of the bodies, I began to see the enemy dead in a new light. The dead occupy a different plane of existence. Even the horribly mangled usually look serene and no longer threatening. The dust covering their open eyes and mouths is the first giveaway. Their letters to and from home, pictures of them in patriotic poses and of sweethearts restored their humanity. They were young too; younger than most of us.

I was elated at our success. So were my troops. We took pleasure at the twisted bloody bodies. Some of the guys took pictures and picked up souvenirs. My senior NCOs and I took pains to ensure that no one mutilated the enemy dead as was rumored to have happened elsewhere following other battles. I took an NVA belt with a star buckle and a Chinese SKS rifle. Later, when I came home not wanting to risk getting caught smuggling in a weapon, I brought only the bayonet.

As the sun rose higher, the bodies began to swell. It reminded me of pictures of the dead at Gettysburg and other Civil War battlefields. It did not take long for the bodies to burst and start to smell. I had read and heard tell of how the mix of different emotions like excitement and elation overcame the fear of battle. Now, satisfied that we had gleaned all we could from the battlefield, we evacuated our wounded and the captured NVA, left the dead where they lay and returned to Wunder Beach. At the time it never occurred to me to ask or even wonder who would bury them.

There is one footnote to this story. 1st Sergeant Paige, who was never comfortable outside the wire became extremely agitated when Mac told him that he would have to return to the Beach on the ground with the rest of the troop. In a fit of rage, he threw his 45-caliber pistol against the bulkhead of an ACAV. It discharged. The bullet hit him in the stomach, and he got his wish to fly back to Wunder Beach via medevac helicopter. Eventually the local field hospital sent him to Japan for further treatment and recovery.

The cloud over the unfortunate departure of 1st SGT Paige bore a silver lining. Master Sergeant Peter B Walker, recently assigned to Squadron headquarters as an operations specialist, was diverted to A Troop as its new First Sergeant. Top Walker was a soldier's soldier. He enlisted in the Jim Crow Army shortly after WWII and served in Germany in a segregated Black tank destroyer unit where he and PSG Fulton became friends. Later, when I became A Troop XO, I learned more about Fulton and the Old Army. Picking up where Fulton left off, Walker taught me how to be a more effective line officer.

First Platoon suffered two additional losses because of Van Phong and Bac Ta. Shortly after we returned to Wunder Beach SSGs "Pappy" Fallus and Miguel Robles found reasons to return to 9th Division HQ at Bear Cat. Apparently, as was common practice following battles, the division reenlistment NCO contacted them offering new assignments in non-combat units.[4] Having seen enough combat, both reenlisted and went immediately to their new unit. I could not begrudge them. They were two good men who never let me or their men down. I never saw Robles again.

---

[4] I first read about this practice in Andrew Wiest's *The Boys of '67: Charlie Company's War in Vietnam*, Osprey Publishing (2012), p. 182. I cannot imagine that this approach to filling reenlistment quotas was unique to the 9th Infantry Division, but the fact that Charlie Company was in a 9th ID battalion surely is more than a coincidence.

Chapter Eight
God Willing and the Creek Don't Rise

The northeast monsoon rains arrived early that year. Normally it rained daily from September through November; it began in mid-August in 1968. Average rainfall in Quang Tri totaled 63.6 inches. Paddies overflowed and rivers and canals frequently came out of their banks. To make matters worse two typhoons slammed I Corps on 6-11 September and 18-24 October causing even more widespread flooding. From the air it looked like the South China Sea inundated all the coastal plain from the beach to the piedmont.

These conditions severely restricted the mobility of 3/5 Cavalry and any attached Infantry units. The flooded paddies and waterway forced our ACAVs and tanks to use established roadways and the Dunes for movement. During and after the monsoons even the roads and most of the Dunes, except for cemeteries, were flooded over and impassable. During those periods we found ourselves restricted to Wunder Beach, Hard Core and cemeteries which afforded some high ground.

Nevertheless, we continued our usual missions like Road Running and cordoning and searching villages along The Street and in the Dunes. Now we even moved into the piedmont to support Infantry units operating there.

On our first foray into the foothills, A Troop moved south along QL1 to the vicinity of LZ Nancy. Nancy suffered a major attack in August when NVA sappers broke through the firebase's defenses on the night of 16 August. We learned later that the attack on Nancy, that coincided with the attack on 1st

Cavalry Division elements around Van Phong, was part of a general NVA/VC post-Tet effort.

This time we took the bridge across the O Giang, the rains had raised its level and widened its banks since August making any thought of another amphibious crossing out of the question. Each platoon took positions on hills around Nancy to block known infiltration routes out of the mountains to the rice growing areas to the east. While we waited it started to rain extremely hard. We moved away from Nancy and back to our own AO. By morning Squadron HQ told us we were in the middle of Typhoon Beth.

We held up on relatively high ground east of Hai Lang. C Troop was stranded in a graveyard unable to move because it had lost three ACAVS. B Troop remained marooned at Hard Core. The rain and lashing wind lasted another forty-eight hours. When it finally stopped, and water levels subsided, B and C Troops made their way back to Wunder Beach, and A Troop returned to Hard Core. It was mostly underwater except for the church, rectory and what had once been a school. Squadron resupplied us with food and fuel via helicopter. We dried out as we waited for the water to subside. In the interim, I had the pleasure of promoting SP4 Terry Reigle AKA "Speedy," TC of A16 to Sargent. I had favored him from my start as platoon leader and depended on him for his savvy and instinct in the field. He was due to DROS in October, so I was glad to have the chance to formally recognize him before he left us.

During our time at Hard Core waiting for the water to go down, an Infantry unit came through the LZ to rest and resupply. The brigade chaplain accompanied them. He arrived carrying the gear of two grunts singing "Oh What a Beautiful Morning" at the top of his lungs and organized a mass followed by a nondenominational service for his troops and others at the base. I had encountered Father Black before and told him I would be marrying a Catholic girl when I got home. He gave me a pre-Cana instruction book and told me to ask any questions next time we met. Later, he sent a certificate of completion to the diocese.

One of the other things we did after the water went down was dispose of ammunition and explosives damaged or deemed unsafe by their inundation during the Great River Crossing and the recent typhoons. That task fell to me as A Troop's demolitions officer. An old bunker complex in Hard

Core, dating from the French-Indochina War, provided the venue. We piled the unsalvageable ammunition and explosives in one of the reinforced concrete pill boxes that made up the bunker complex, packed C4 in and around it, doused the whole pile with diesel fuel and gasoline and wrapped the pile tightly in detcord to ensure instantaneous detonation. The deafening explosion blew out the bunker's walls and lifted its roof some hundred feet into the air. Most of the ammunition and explosives went up with the blast. Small arms ammunition cooked off in the resulting fire for at least an hour. The following day we hosed down the pile and buried what was left. All agreed that we had done good. The only thing we missed was marshmallows.

As the waters continued to subside, things got back to normal. We returned to cordoning fishing villages in the Dunes and farming villages on The Street with the usual mixed results. One day turned up nothing, the next we got eleven bona fide VC and some weapons. Intelligence figured they must have moved into the village to wait out the storm and gotten complacent. Usually, we returned to Wunder Beach or Hard Core around mid-day.

When at the Beach we were finally able to catch up on our maintenance. We soon had all ten of 1st Platoon's vehicles up and running. I must give credit where it is due. In mid-September we got a new platoon sergeant. PSG Becker was on his second tour in Vietnam. As a qualified Armored Cavalry platoon sergeant, he quickly had the guys working effectively on the more mundane tasks associated with their jobs including maintenance. Becker and I soon developed a good working relationship though I never got as close to him as I did with PSG Fulton.

Life on the Beach was not all work and no play. Everyone in the Troop got to spend time at the beach. Since the beginning of monsoon season surf was up. It proved to be especially good for body and air mattress surfing. Those of us with a little body surfing experience took delight in helping the non- and weak swimmers in the troop get comfortable in the water and learn to air mattress surf. Our troop interpreter Hahn picked it up quickly and soon had all of us impressed with his fearlessness and skill in the water.

Our new First Sergeant, Top Peter Walker added to the spirit of the beach scene by moving dinner beach side whenever possible. Despite the frequent rain it seemed that nothing could dampen A Troop's days at the beach.

Wunder Beach Party L to R Griffith, Goree, Meaders, Calior

However, cookouts on the beach took the troop's morale only so far. I attended to the platoon's esprit. With the support of the platoon NCOs, PSG Becker and I obtained some black berets and outfitted everyone in them. We used the 9th Infantry Division patch as the flash on which every man displayed his rank. My intent was that we would wear the berets only when in formation, which we did, once. The Squadron Commander found out and put the kibosh on the whole Idea.

I was more successful in my second effort to boost morale in the platoon. We had taken a lot of ribbing over our river crossing exploits in August. Jo helped me design and made up cards and certificates for each member of the ACAVs that sank that day and authorized them to paint yellow submarines on their tracks just below the identification insignia. It was a hit. I soon received requests from other platoons and Troops that lost vehicles crossing rivers for copies of the certificate and induction into the "Mysterious and Sacred order of the Yellow Submarine". Squadron did not raise an objection. The Sergeant Major even requested a copy of the certificate for his files. (See Appendix II)

Yellow Submarine

LZ Hard Core. Waiting for the flood to recede

The rains continued through all of this and added to growing rumors that the Squadron would soon move. That decision had already been made with respect to the supply depot at Wunder Beach. With typhoons threatening to completely submerge the Wunder Beach – Hai Lang road, it became clear that Wunder Beach had served its purpose. The arrival of a second typhoon in mid-October proved even worse. The rivers and canals overflowed and flooded the rice paddies again and water undermined and cut the only road between Hard Core and the Beach. The river also lifted the bridge at Hard Core off its abutments making movement of armored vehicles and heavy transport trucks impossible until the engineers could repair it.

At the end of the month the squadron received orders to move south, not back to the Delta as was planned, to Camp Evans, a brigade size fire base some thirty kilometers south in the piedmont west of QL1. This move brought the squadron under operational control of the 101st Airborne Division.

The move coincided with another change for A Troop. In anticipation of a return south, squadron sent Captain Mac south as part of an advance party to plan and coordinate the relocation. We never saw him again. Our new troop commander was Captain Dave Meaders the Squadron S2. Like me, Meaders had served in the Sixth ACR, though in a different squadron, before coming to Vietnam so we could relate on similar experiences. Still, it took all of us a while to adjust to his command practices.

AFTER ACTION REPORT FOR PERIOD OF OPERATIONS OF OPCON TO 1ST CAVALRY DIVISION (AIRMOBILE), 17 MAY 1968 TO 7 NOV 1968.

Chapter Nine
Camp Evans

Helicopters returning to Camp Evans

Camp Evans lay in the piedmont just to the west of QL1 about halfway between Hue and Quang Tri. Set in gently rolling hills at about fifty feet above mean sea level. The Marines constructed it late in 1966. The 1st Cavalry Division (Airmobile) took over the base in January 1968 and in turn transferred it to the 2nd Brigade, 101st Airborne Division later in 1968. Units based at Evans included an infantry battalion, a field artillery battalion, an assault helicopter battalion, an ARA artillery company, a signal battalion, and a surgical hospital. The camp also had an 8,775-foot dirt runway that accommodated C130 transport planes and Air Force tactical air support aircraft.[5]

Camp Evans was basically circular in design. The runway and revetments for helicopters and other aircraft occupied the center. Concentrically out from the aviation facilities were maintenance and support units followed by housing for troops. A dirt road ringed the compound which was in turn surrounded by an earthen berm, concertina wire and a cleared area about 100 yards wide interlaced with more wire, mines and obstacles covered by concealed machine gun posts roughly fifty yards apart backed up by multi story sandbagged strong points that could bathe each sector in light with communications to each machine gun post, adjacent strong points and a central camp security headquarters. Tenant units manned the security perimeter on a rotating basis.

Housing for units consisted of canvas platform tents stretched on wooden frames. Each tent accommodated platoon-sized units of roughly thirty men each. A company of infantry or troop of cavalry might take up to six tents for platoon and headquarters troops, an administration tent and a supply and armorers' tent. Altogether, this represented a major upgrade in living conditions for 3/5 Cavalry troopers used to living on their tracks night to night in the field or in a base camp.

None of this happened right away of course. The sudden departure from Wunder Beach and environs and the necessity of coordinating with the departing 1st Cavalry Division and arrival of the 101st Airborne Division caught all parties involved unprepared for the change. Space had to be identified for each line troop, headquarters troop, squadron headquarters, maintenance, supply and messing facilities. Even as general decisions were made regarding location and distribution of assets, they were not ready for occupation.

Squadron's solution to this dilemma was to park the line troops outside the gate while headquarter elements moved in and prepared to receive the rest of us.

Rather than simply park us outside the gate, Squadron dispersed the troops in blocking positions on a line stretching from My Chanh in the west eastward to the river O Lau. The purpose of this activity was to permit ARVN and local RFPF units to flush any VC from the villages into our forces. We sat on this line for nearly two weeks without any contact while we waited to get into our new digs at Camp Evans.

---

[5] https://en.wikipedia.org/wiki/Camp_Evans_(Vietnam).

A Troop occupied about a kilometer of the line with two platoons abreast and one in reserve with the CO as a reaction force. The terrain was not unlike the Dunes of our former AO, less sandy with more scrub and intermittent ponds draining south to north into the river O Giang and its tributary canals and streams. The intermittent ponds varied in depth forming unfordable obstacles between our ACAVs and Tanks. At night they presented potential threats to platoons online as VC could infiltrate between the tracks via them. This necessitated 360-degree security around each track requiring trip flares and mines all around. We also had to keep our ACAV ramps up and maintain blackout conditions from dusk to dawn.

During daylight hours the Troop conducted searches of the surrounding area for weapons and rice caches as well as foot patrols into the villages and hamlets to our front. These operations turned up little, adding to the tedium of our existence. With the monsoon tapering, the days became hot, muggy, and dusty. Absent the ability to use the beach or base camp improvised showers and laundries, we became more dirty and grubbier.

Charlie remained in the area. One day, after a routine foray into the dunes, we reoccupied the cordon. As A16 pulled into a new position, I hopped off and moved around the track to make sure the rest of the platoon lined up properly. Suddenly, I stepped into a hole and fell over. It turned out to be a booby trapped 105mm high explosive artillery round. But for a rusty wire I would have been blown to kingdom come or at least severely maimed. Initially, I took it in stride. After we cleared the area and blew the round in place, creating a crater three feet deep by five feet in diameter, I sat down on the ramp and pondered how close I had come to becoming a meaningless statistic of the war and the random nature of it. Twice in the previous five months I sustained slight wounds and remained in the field. On the two occasions that I should have been blown away, I came away without a scratch. Now. Shaking uncontrollably, I remained on the ramp pondering the meaning of the event. I listened to my then favorite songs: Judy Collins' "Send in the Clowns," and Mary Hopkins' "Those Were the Days." I spoke to no one, and no one spoke to me.

Once during this period, we caught a break. A USO mini show dropped in on an artillery battery supporting the cordon, and we were invited. The show consisted of Tippi Hedren, the actress and comedian Joey Bishop, backed by a small band. A Troop arrived in a cloud of dust too late for the show, but in time for a meet and greet with the headliners. When my turn came Bishop threw his arm around me and in his classic deadpan cracked, "You need to stop chewing that thing (my mustache) and let it grow some more." As far as I was concerned that legitimized it enough to wear it while I remained in the field.

Author and Joey Bishop

New developments soon took my mind off my mortality. Word came down from Squadron HQ that we were going to have a Command Maintenance Management Inspection (CMMI). This, along with the Annual General Inspection (AGI), perturbated every level of a line unit's activity and represented the bane of every soldier's existence. For us in A Troop it began with a directive to get rid of all extraneous equipment, luxury items and off load a layer of ammunition from our tracks. The objective of this exercise was to render the vehicles to "combat ready" status. That meant turning in or discarding cots, hammocks, sleeping matts, books, magazines, and pinups; items that made the troopers' existence bearable. We had previously addressed the ammunition issue. Extra ammunition represented a security blanket of which we never had enough.

An unintended consequence of this Chinese Fire Drill was a trip into Camp Evans where we stashed all the personal gear in the platoon's tent and the ammunition in a storage container and began three days of intensive maintenance on the tracks in the motor pool, a relatively level dirt field large enough to accommodate all A Troop's vehicles and equipment.

Colonel Grills came through the motor pool one morning and expressed his displeasure with our progress. The ramps of our ACAVs and the fenders of our tanks were muddy, and our tool bags were dirty! I also learned through Major Ray Bell, the squadron XO that the Colonel was none too pleased with my appearance. The CO's words according to Bell were, "that God Damned Lt Griffith, one of the best platoon leaders in the squadron, but if it isn't a raggedy bush hat, it's a raggedy moustache!" I promised the XO that I would trim it before I left for R&R.

Sometime during this period, the subject of dogs came up. GIs loved dogs. Perhaps that was because they viewed dogs as kindred spirits who shared the privations of soldering with them. All the troops in 3/5 Cavalry had at least one dog. A Troop had several most sired by 2nd Platoon's Bozo. Bozo fell at Van Phong when he was caught between crossfire when C Troop joined the attack against the NVA. His legacy lived on through at least two litters of puppies from Dorris, the medics' mascot. 1st Platoon acquired one named "Gee Whiz." We were forced to put him down when he got into something that made him violently sick. Somehow Colonel Grills got wind of this and decreed that all the line troops limit themselves to one dog. Major Bell spread the word and took the heat for the unpopular order.

We finished the CMMI (I have no memory of how it turned out) and took on a new but familiar mission, Road Running QL1 from My Chan in the north to the bridge over the Song Bo south of Evans. Two platoons shared the Road Runner mission while the third presided over a sector of the Camp Evans perimeter. Our first time out proved a little hairy. My new driver on A16 lost sight of the track ahead of us, miscalculated a turn and left the road at 20mph. The road bank was steep, and if the ground had been hard instead of soft, we probably would have rolled. The road ran adjacent to a defended bridge, and we also drove over a roll of barbed concertina wire. It took two ACAVs to pull us out and about forty-five minutes to cut the wire out of the tracks, sprocket, and road wheels. All in a night's work.

Road Running could be tedious and tiring. The round trip from Evans north to My Chan then south to the Song Bo and back to Evans was about fifty miles. An uneventful trip of about two hours left little time for rest between runs. To break the monotony, we sometimes resorted to playing practical jokes on Headquarters staff. Paul Fussell referred to staff as "the enemy in the rear" and noted the almost universal animosity between staff and line troops in WWI.[6] So it was that one night that John Calior, Second Platoon leader and I cooked up a story about a train off the tracks and blocking QL1 near My Chan. There was a north-south railroad paralleling QL1, but no trains had run on it north of Hue for years. The operations officer in the TOC took down my report and requested details. I elaborated that an ARVN platoon was on the train, and through one of the men who spoke English, we were able to persuade the engineer to uncouple the cars and move them off the road. That allowed us to continue the mission. At the same time, I alerted John that one of the cars still partially blocked the highway and that he should be aware of it. Squadron dutifully recorded it all and asked that we provide updates whenever we passed that point.

At daybreak John closed out the tale reporting that a wrecker train came up and lifted the cars back on the tracks enabling the train to move on. We found the whole "incident" to be hilarious and indicative of how clueless and gullible some rear echelon people could be about the situation outside the wire. The operations officer never questioned the report and passed it to Squadron HQ. From there it went on to Brigade and probably Division HQ.[7]

By now I was getting to the end of my time as platoon leader. I was due for R&R and Squadron brought me in to clean up, trim my moustache and make my way to Saigon to go and meet Jo for six days in Hawaii.

---

[6] Paul Fussell, *The Great War and Modern Memory*, Oxford University Press reprint 1979, pp. 81-82.
[7] The operations officer on duty that night turned out to be Tom Emerson, my West Point classmate. I never told him he had been the butt of our joke. After his time in the TOC, Tom joined A Troop as a platoon leader. He died in a fire fight on the DMZ later in 1969.

Chapter Ten
R&R

After completing one month of service in Vietnam, every soldier was entitled to a week of R&R in one of several places: Hawaii; Sidney, Australia; Bangkok, Thailand; Hong Kong; Kuala Lumpur, Malaysia; Manila, Philippines; Singapore; Taipei, Taiwan; or Tokyo, Japan. Hawaii was highest on the list of married soldiers, Bangkok most favored by single men. One applied for R&R and received orders to go based on availability. On assignment you were removed from your unit, cleaned up and sent to a center for transportation to your destination.[8]

Jo and I started planning for R&R almost as soon as I got to A Troop. We hoped to meet in Hawaii as close to Christmas as possible, about halfway through my tour and during her grad school holiday break. Because 3/5 Cavalry was far from 9th Division HQ, I had to time my application to coincide with the monthly publication of available slots. This took more than routine communication between Squadron and Division to assure my assignment. At the same time Jo and I had to time her travel to Hawaii so that we arrived on the same date.

The least expensive way for Jo to get from Worcester to Hawaii involved joining a tour. That got her to Hawaii a day ahead of me. She remembers sustaining herself on leftovers from other tour members' meals and raw fruit from local trees. After I arrived, she skipped out of the group until it was time to go back. It also gave us a place to store our stuff while we moved around the Islands.

---

[8] TOD Advisor's Notebook, Essay4-R&R.htm#Top pp. 1-5, passim. See also, "R&R" in Honolulu a Six-Day Moment of Peace for Soldiers and Their Wives., NYT, April 13, 1970, p. 35.

We spent the first couple of days in Honolulu doing touristy things like shopping for Christmas gifts. It seemed surreal wandering around the city and shopping malls decorated in traditional holiday fashion with carols wafting from loudspeakers.

We took in singer Don Ho's show featuring "Tiny Bubbles," and bought the obligatory "Suck 'em Up" glasses that came with the drinks; one round per set. Ho was a real showman. He recognized all the R&R people in the audience (about half) and tailored his patter to us. The show included some traditional Hawaiian music and dancing with audience participation. Luckily, I escaped being dragged onstage, fitted with a grass skirt, and being instructed in dancing the hula. It was all in good fun.

The next day we joined Jo's cousin Kay and her husband Nip Akona at the Outrigger and Canoe Club, well known for its dedication to the preservation and advancement of ancient Hawaiian water sports of surfing and outrigger canoeing, prominently located on Waikiki Beach. After lunch, Nip took us out for a ride in one of the Club's outriggers. Looking back, I realize that was one of the highpoints of our time in Hawaii.

From Oahu, we island hopped to Maui and drove from Lahaina, once a whaling port and first capitol of the Kingdom of Hawaii, to Kaanapali Beach. At the time only one hotel graced the Beach, a far cry from what since became a complex of five resort hotels and six condominiums. Despite rain, our only bad weather day, I had to try out the surf. Body surfing at Kaanapali equaled that at Wunder Beach where we had lifeguards of sorts. Jo did not like the high surf and called me out of the water quickly. The weather grew worse forcing us to curtail sightseeing, so we moved on to the Big Island the next day.

On Hawaii we rented a car and drove around the island. We saw Akaka Falls, walked on Punalu'u Black Sand Beach, and went through Volcanos National Park ending up at the National Park Service Lodge overlooking Kilauea Caldera. I was especially taken by the foreboding painting of Pele, goddess of fire, rising from her home in Kilauea.

We flew back to Oahu that night arriving late and exhausted. The next day, our last of my R&R, Jo and I celebrated an early Christmas. She set up a miniature tree which we decorated and piled presents for each other and family at home underneath; a bittersweet moment.

Next morning, we said our goodbyes and I went back to the R&R center and shortly thereafter to the plane back to Vietnam. Unlike the flight from

Vietnam, which was loud and boisterous, the mood on the way back was somber. A few of us shared memories, but for the most part we remained lost in our thoughts.

All too soon we were back at Ton Son Nhut where we quickly recovered our fatigues and weapons and returned to our units. It took me three days via hops to Danang and Camp Evans. I was back in time for Christmas.

Chapter Eleven
A Troop XO

I got to spend a few days with outgoing XO Jim Bursitis, aka Brutus, and quickly learned there was a lot more to the job of troop executive officer than I thought. Since the Troop CO spent most of his time in the field directing the line platoons it was up to the XO to keep everything running in the rear. That included administration, maintenance, mess, and property. On paper that looks straight forward; in practice a myriad of details and realities complicated the task. I was already well acquainted with the challenges of maintenance. Keeping my platoon's ten vehicles running and combat ready was never easy. Now including the thirty tracks of the three line platoons I had responsibility for Headquarters Platoon's tracks, trucks and Jeeps including some unauthorized trucks that were brought along when the troop moved north the previous year.

The fact that we had unauthorized vehicles as well as assorted unauthorized equipment became clear to me as I conducted a mandatory inventory of everything in the troop. Normally the CO was responsible for troop property. But as noted above, in Vietnam that fell to the XO. Accordingly, I started a total inventory. Regulations held that we identify what we had and did not have against the list of what we should have. It started with the big stuff (tanks and ACAVs) and went all the way down to little stuff such as tents, typewriters, tools and mess equipment like pots, pans, and field stoves. Personal weapons issued individually to soldiers were in a class by themselves. Once completed and reconciled with the master list maintained by the Squadron Property Book Officer, we then had to decide what to do about surpluses and shortages.

Surplus equipment was tolerated if it contributed to the mission. Some Scouts, for example, preferred the AK47 to the M16 because it could take more punishment and continue to function when fouled compared to the more finely machined M16. American soldiers also knew that the enemy could be put off guard when fired on by an AK47. Shortages presented a different challenge. Signatories were required to make up shortages. Since no one wanted to get stuck having to make up for unaccounted equipment, units resorted to some artful solutions to balance the books.

3/5 Cavalry units, both the squadron and troops, kept two sets of books. After a battle or incident during which equipment was lost or destroyed, the troop involved would report losses from its shortage list. Sometimes squadron told the troop what to declare lost. For example, on one occasion after an NVA/VC rocket destroyed an empty CONEX container, Squadron got together with a couple of line troops to fill that container with equipment enabling the units in question to request that the lost items be replaced. A more egregious example occurred when a tank had a suspension so badly worn that squadron maintenance could not repair it. When the unfortunate tank ran over a mine it was declared combat lost and therefor replaced.

The easiest way to make up equipment shortages was by "midnight requisition." When the 1st Brigade 5th Mechanized Infantry landed at Wunder Beach, 3/5 Cavalry troopers quickly made their way through the Mech's motor pool scrounging anything not tied down. One of that unit's officers complained to 1st Sergeant Paige and said a guard almost shot one of the thieves. The 1st Sergeant replied, "It couldn't have been one of my men, sir, he would have shot back."

One compensation to being XO was having a real cot and always sleeping through the night under cover. At some point, A Troop got an extra platoon size cabin which enabled us to move 1st Sergeant Walker and the administrative clerks into their own space along with the supply sergeant and armorer. I took over the vacated space and turned it into sleeping quarters for me, the troop CO, and the platoon leaders. Since they were usually in the field, I had the place pretty much to myself.

Each cabin had a bunker next to it to provide safe cover during mortar or rocket attacks. These were left over from the time when the 1st Cav Division occupied Camp Evans. I did not pay much attention to them until the night of our first rocket attack. At around 0200 hours the camp siren started wailing; the lights went out simultaneously. That alerted us that an attack was imminent. At about the same time, I heard the whoosh of a rocket passing overhead. Not waiting further, I dashed out of the hut and into the bunker, smacking my forehead on the lintel and stumbling sideways into about half a foot of cold muddy water. That did it for the night. Satisfied that the threat had passed, I crawled out of the bunker, and back in the hut. I found some dry fatigues and socks, pulled them on and went back to sleep.

In the morning Top and I inspected the area. We decided that the bunkers needed attention and agreed to assign a detail to do just that. Our plan was overtaken by events. After breakfast, the men quietly set to work shoring up the sandbag sides and overheads of the bunkers and bailing them out. Over time we learned to recognize the sound of rockets coming at us or passing overhead and acting accordingly. Taking a more fatalistic attitude, I never went to the bunker again.

Except for the occasional rocket attack, the war did not intrude on us. Combat operations began shifting west into the mountains and the Cambodian border leaving us in the rear with the mundane chores. The exception involved Road Running missions that the squadron conducted regularly. In addition to keeping the highway between Hue and My Chan clear at night, cavalry troops and their platoons periodically did daylight cordon and search operations into villages on either side of the highway. These actions disrupted local VC activity, but also resulted in American casualties when, for example, an ACAV or tank carrying infantrymen struck a mine or rolled over on steep terrain wounding or otherwise injuring passengers and crew. Night ambushes especially plagued Road Runners. One night in January, a 2nd Platoon ACAV hit a command detonated mine near Phong Dien. Casualties were quickly evacuated to the 18th Surgical Hospital right at Camp Evans. They called us immediately to tell us and added that one of the killed was an officer. When the troop had casualties, it fell to the XO or the 1st Sargent to identify the dead and visit the wounded. After seven months in Vietnam, I never got used to the task. Top and I hopped in my jeep and raced over to the MASH. After checking on the wounded I turned to the dead. A corpsman informed me there were two; one was a lieutenant. *This was different.* There was only one officer in a cavalry platoon, the platoon leader. Combat bonds soldiers tightly. Before becoming troop XO, I had led first platoon. John, the second platoon leader and I had supported one another in many fights. We were fast friends. I never had to identify the body of a friend before.

LONG AGO AND FAR AWAY • 65

On the floor of the dimly lit, musty morgue tent lay two stretchers containing poncho-covered bodies. I hesitated. Finally, sweating and trembling, I forced myself forward and made a positive I.D. of the enlisted trooper. More slowly, I moved to the remaining body. I drew back the poncho and investigated the lifeless, round freckled face of an army lieutenant. *It was not John!* In relief and disbelief, I stared at the body. He was very fair, almost pretty. His eyes were closed, and his expression was serene. There was no sign of violence or pain on the exposed part of his body. He looked vaguely familiar, but he had no dog tags or wallet. His uniform was new, so new that it bore no name tag or unit patch. "He's not mine," I said tersely and returned to the living. Another unit identified and claimed his body later that day. I never learned his name. I never forgot his face.

On Memorial Day 1984, still on active duty, I was stationed in Washington. Early in the morning I drove into D.C. where the Vietnam Unknown lay in state in the Capitol Rotunda. Even at that hour the line was long, and it moved slowly. Memories that I had not recalled in years resurfaced. When I reached the head of the line and confronted the flag-draped, gunmetal coffin I was back in that field morgue. The image of that baby-faced lieutenant came clearly to mind. *"I know you!"* I thought. *"Welcome home."*

I left quickly and drove to the Vietnam Veteran's Memorial. I visited "my guys," Fulton and Sizemore, the names of classmates and other soldiers I had served with who died in the war. But my thoughts were on the Unknown soon to be buried at Arlington. For me he would forever have the face of that nameless lieutenant back in Vietnam. His name was on the wall along with those of the fifty-odd others who died or had been reported missing-in-action the same day. I was wrong back then. He *was* one of mine. He was my Unknown Soldier. He still is.[9]

The following day it was back to business as usual. Top and I assigned details to perform several tasks. First, we sent five men and a truck to Sector White (Camp Perimeter Defense) to work on bunkers, four men with a truck to move the ammunition storage point (ASP), four mechanics to build a new tool room, two mechanics to prepare A23 for turn-in, and the remaining mechanics to work on track maintenance. Then I realized we had forgotten trash

---

[9] In 1998 the Vietnam Unknown Soldier was identified as Air Force LT Michael J Blassie and reburied in the National Cemetery at Jefferson Barracks. *NYT*, 30 June 1998, p A1. In the process of researching this memoir, I was able to identify my Unknown Soldier as Army LT Ronald Michels.

pickup. So, I pulled the ASP detail off that job and send them on the trash run. The Squadron XO called to tell me that I must clear out of our motor pool because the unit moving in would be arriving a month early. I called in all details and put them to work clearing the old area and levied four men from 3rd Platoon to help. That suspended all work on Sector White and the ASP.

Meanwhile, 2nd Platoon came in unannounced and proceeded to strip A23 of usable parts without replacing them with bad ones. I could not turn in the track stripped. Simultaneously, Squadron called to request our VTR to recover a deadlined ACAV; there went my tool room builders and movers. I learned about A23, but 2nd Platoon had moved back out before I could do anything about the pilferage. Squadron called to cancel the VTR request which 1st Platoon requested almost immediately. Lastly, Captain Meaders called in to tell me A Troop had a change of mission, and, oh by the way, "How are things going?" It was 11:30 hours, and I had not accomplished a thing that we set out to do. Thus, be it ever.

Things turned a little better in the afternoon. The NCO inspecting A23 for turn in took one look at it and said, "You've got to be shitting me!" He accepted it anyway along with a rain suit and a bottle of scotch.

Our need for replacement parts and equipment, especially tools for our tracks, became more acute as the supply system backed up. I decided to go on a scrounging trip to Danang. Someone I met on my way back from R&R (I cannot remember who) worked at the supply depot there and told me if I ever needed anything to give him a call. I did and sketched our needs to him. He asked me what we had to trade and told me to "come on down." SSG Berry, head of troop maintenance, Top and I ransacked the Troop for souvenirs (VC/NVA weapons and equipment), and Berry and I were on our way.

We drove to Danang in my semi open jeep in cold, wet, and foggy weather. QL1 was paved the whole way, and the roadsides were cleared of vegetation about twenty-five to thirty meters on each side. We moved around backed up convoys to go as fast as possible. The mountains closed in from the right eventually going directly to the sea north of Danang. The only way to the city was over the mountains via Hai Van Pass. We climbed up the mountain on a series of precipitous switchbacks not unlike those you encounter crossing the Alps; no guard rails to prevent you from skidding off the road and down steep banks. At the top of the pass stood an old monastery from which a path led to an overlook of the mountain and the sea. Not interested in sightseeing we plunged down from the pass on another series of switchbacks arriving on the outskirts of Danang at dusk. The trip took five and a half hours; today it takes two via a tunnel that bypasses the climb altogether.

Road to Danang

The Danang trip proved to be wildly successful. Line troops would have considered the city a paradise. I wore my best fatigues and boots and still drew stares. We felt like a couple of country bumpkins visiting the big city for the first time. We got enough surplus equipment to outfit two tracks. Our scrounging contacts promised us enough parts and sundry equipment to fill two more vehicles. Between SSG Berry and I we hit all three exchanges filling friends' shopping lists. We decided to come back the following week with a truck.

The trip back to Evans was as uneventful as it was spectacular. Clear cloudless skies revealed the panoramic view of the mountains and the sea as well as bucolic fishing villages and rice farming activities along the route. We got back to our base without slowing down once.

On our second trip we arrived with more souvenirs, extensive shopping lists and the truck. Our friends took the truck to the depot while we went to the exchanges again. Our lists mostly consisted of cigars, cigarettes, canned foods, and booze. I also bought a couple of cases of frozen steaks that I assumed would be defrosted by the time we got back to Evans. When we returned to the depot our truck was ready. It contained several unmarked crates which I was advised not to open until we got back.

After an uneventful return we pulled into A Troop's motor pool. First, we gave the steaks to the Mess Sergeant. Then we opened the two biggest crates. They contained the Basic Issue Items (BII) for two M48 tanks, just what we were looking for. There was one small problem. They were for *Marine Corps* tanks. The Marines used an older model M48. Not all the parts were compatible with ours. In the classic tradition of Army scrounging, we kept what we could use, such as tools, and got rid of the rest. This was one of those, "I don't care how you do it Sergeant, just do it," solutions, that young officers never learned in school. This ended my last scrounging trip to DaNang but not my last trip there.

Chapter Twelve
Surgery and Convalescence

There I was, minding my own business while taking a shower when I noticed a lump in my right groin. I pushed at it and it went back into my body. It did not hurt but protruded again when I released it. After talking with the Squadron surgeon, I went over to the 18th Surgical Hospital and asked one of the doctors there to look at it. "Yup, you've got one," he said, "an inguinal hernia, i.e., a rupture. It's too bad we can't do elective surgery here," he continued, "I love to do hernias." I would have to go to the 95th Evacuation Hospital at DaNang.

CPT Meaders and I left for DaNang on February 22, he to begin R&R and I for surgery. Neither of us is clear on how we got there, though we do remember finding lodging at the 3rd Marine Amphibious Force headquarters BOQ and getting kicked out of the dining room there, a closed mess not unlike the one I enjoyed while at Ft. Story, because we were too scruffy. A marine corps general or navy admiral overheard the commotion, interceded, and made the manager seat and feed us on his account.

The next day we went our separate ways. I was back at Camp Evans on the 24th. The previous day NVA/VC hit DaNang, among around 100 other targets, causing mass casualties.[10] The hospital would not admit me but assured me it would do so if I returned on March 1. Meanwhile, I continued to do XO things like driving up to Con Tien, where B and C Troops were so I could pay those A troopers still on our personnel roster. This was my first time so close to the DMZ, just two miles to the north.

---

[10] This was the beginning of a N Vietnamese offensive known as Tet 1969, a series of attacks focused mostly on Saigon and DaNang. https://en.wikipedia.org/wiki/Tet_1969

Con Tien was a heavily fortified piece of high ground among a string of strong points that stretched from the coast to the Laotian border. From it we could see with the naked eye North Vietnamese trucks bringing ammunition to enemy artillery batteries in the DMZ. We could not fire into the DMZ unless fired upon first because of the bombing halt then in place as part of the peace talks. That did not prevent the NVA from aggressively running patrols south of the DMZ where they frequently ran into our defensive patrols. Strange war.

On March 2 I caught a helicopter hop to DaNang and was quickly admitted to the 95th Evac, prepped and taken off all food and drink until twelve hours after surgery. They took me into the OR at 0730 the next morning and put me to sleep; I was back in the ward by 1000. I tried to walk around 1300 but apparently the medication had not worn off causing me to be quite sick. The head nurse on the ward caught me and threw me back into bed with orders to "stay." For the next two days they kept me on a liquid diet and watched my every attempt to get out of bed and walk.

The patients in my forty-person ward represented a cross section of the war: U.S., ARVN and NVA/VC soldiers, civilian men, women, the elderly, children, and babies. It got especially interesting when the babies started to cry. There was one three-year-old girl who came from an abandoned village with shrapnel in her leg. She was filthy, covered with lice and terrified. They kept her on the ward and in time the nurses, orderlies and patients spoiled her rotten. Eventually they sent her to a nearby orphanage.

The Catholic Chaplin at the 95th was an honest to God Irishman. He joined the US Army because he wanted to serve in Vietnam. While making his rounds one day he noticed Jo's name on a letter I was about to mail and offered her his blessing that the "wind be always at your back." Strange world.

My stitches came out on March 9, and the 95th transferred me immediately to an Air Force unit for transport to a recovery center. About twenty of us filled the ward. That afternoon the corpsmen treated us to ice cream and a movie: *The Odd Couple*, starring Jack Lemmon and Walter Matthau. We appreciated the show despite its unintended consequences. Imagine grown men laughing so hard that they had tears in their eyes as they burst stitches left and right. The next day they loaded us on ambulance planes. I made sure that they did not put me on the plane to Japan. Rumor had it that if you went to Japan, you would not get credit for a full tour in Vietnam but would be eligible for redeployment after six months.

They put me on the plane to the Sixth Convalescent Center (6th C C) at Cam Ranh Bay, a little over an hour south of DaNang. There, I went to a ward housing twenty odd men, who, like me needed physical rehabilitation before they could be released back to their units. This enabled the Army hospital system to free up beds in the surgical or evacuation hospitals without having to send recovering patients out of the country thereby losing them for further duty and requiring replacements.

The ward was a standard Army barrack built of plywood with rollup canvass sidewalls surrounded by sandbags. There were no sandbag bunkers. We were told that in the event of an attack we should roll out of our beds onto the floor and stay put until hospital staff and security personnel gave us further directions. Besides, they reassured us, Cam Ranh Bay was far removed from any area of combat and had never been attacked. It was the safest place in Vietnam.[11]

I quickly settled into the patients' routine:

> **0700 – get up, make bed, sweep floor, shave.**
> **0730 – breakfast.**
> **0930 – coffee call.**
> **1200 – dinner.**
> **1700 – supper.**

I got fifteen minutes of physical therapy daily and saw the doctor on Tuesday and Friday. There were no other requirements. I spent the day reading, going to the beach or napping. Sometimes I went to the nightly movies.

The 6th CC had a MARS (Military Affiliate Radio System) station from which staff and patients could call home. You had to book calls in advance and limit them to five minutes. You could not just pick up a phone and make a long-distance call with MARS. You had to use radio-telephone procedure, pausing, and saying "OVER" so the other party could speak. I called Jo and my family. Both connections were bad, so I could not understand anyone very well, but it really was the idea of talking to someone at home that counted.

I spent a lot of time at the beach. It had beautiful white sand and occasional surf, but I was not ready to try body surfing yet, even though the surf at Cam

---

[11] In fact, sapper attacks in Aug '69, killed two patients and wounded sixty-three.

Ranh Bay proved to be much tamer than Wunder Beach. We did get out on the water once, courtesy of the Red Cross. They took all the ambulatory patients on a day cruise around the facility. The highlight for me was seeing the hulk of a WWII Japanese destroyer sunk by our navy towards the end of that war. I knew Cam Ranh Bay was prized as a deep-water port. After we left Vietnam, the Soviet Union and then Russia leased space there for both its navy and air force.

The 6th CC discharged me on March 29 with orders that I remain on light duty for four to six weeks. I got back to A Troop the very next day and have no memory of how I did so. My letters to Jo tell me that by March 31, I was at Dong Ha, the Troop Base camp finishing the pay roll much as I had the month before I left.

Things had changed in the time I was gone. A Troop joined the rest of the Squadron at the DMZ as soon as Captain Meaders returned from R&R. Almost immediately they got into a heavy firefight with an NVA unit trying to move into the neutral zone below the boarder. The toll came to eleven tracks lost, five killed and thirty-two wounded. My West Point classmate Tom Emerson, 2nd Platoon leader, was among the dead. I also learned that another classmate was killed around the same time. As if to balance the scale I learned that two friends with whom I had close ties had recently become fathers. The war brought many bittersweet ironies.

One additional bit of news awaited my return. I received alert orders that my next assignment would be in Germany. That news really agitated Jo and my correspondence with her for the coming weeks as we were just getting to cases on plans for our wedding as soon as I returned from Vietnam. Meanwhile, the Squadron Commander, LTC Thomas Carpenter, had to decide what to do with me for my final two months of duty, half of which had to be on light duty.

Chapter Thirteen
Squadron Staff

Major Nicholas Krawciw, Squadron XO and the CO, Lieutenant Colonel Thomas Carpenter, both of whom instructed me at West Point, decided to appoint me Assistant S-3 (Operations Officer) in charge of the day-to-day management of the Tactical Operations Center (TOC). But first, MAJ K directed me to set up and take charge of a Jump CP (Command Post) at Vandergrift Combat Base in support of Squadron activities along QL9 running west from Dong Ha into Laos.

    Because the mission took our troops to the site of the former combat base at Khe Sanh, 3/5 Cavalry needed a relay station to monitor and forward communications between the forward units and Squadron HQ. Since we already had a logistics unit forward deployed at Vandergrift, it made sense to collocate the Jump CP there. Subsequently, I took an M577 Command Post Vehicle with a crew of four and we drove to Vandergrift. The trip there took us out of the rolling foothills around Dong Ha into mountain country that in many places struck me as surreal. Past a landmark known as the Rockpile, the highway turned south and wound through a steep narrow valley (great ambush territory) to Vandergrift that lay astride QL9.

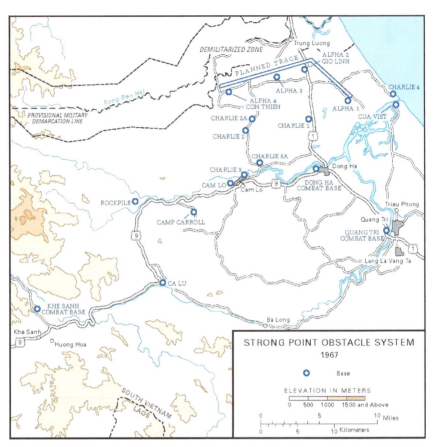

MAP 3 - DMZ - Strong Points Obstacle System, 1967. Source: CMH Pub 91-6-1. MACV THE JOINT COMMAND IN THE YEARS OF ESCALATION, 1962-1967 (2007) p. 424. Note: This map depicts the proposed McNamara Line and shows the road network, base camps and fire bases across the DMZ through 1972.

My first task after setting up the CP involved establishing communications with the forward elements of the Squadron and HQ back at Dong Ha. We also had until midnight to change all call signs and radio frequencies with which I had not been provided. Thus, HQ had to send them to us by code. Simultaneously, we learned that an ARVN unit adjacent to our forward elements had set out ambushes nearby. This required our units to relocate their night positions and ambush sites after dark, plot and call them in to Squadron HQ.

All of this took place amidst fire and exploding debris from the logistics support area where a Marine CH47 helicopter crashed early in the evening causing a fire that spread to the fuel and ammunition sites. Jim Bursitis, formerly of A Troop, who was running the Squadron forward supply point, about 200 meters from the crash site, took a couple of M113 logistics tracks into the area and rescued Marines trapped there. Jim was awarded the Soldiers Medal for his quick reaction and bravery.

The operation west toward Kea Sanh netted nothing save another Yellow Submarine for 1st Platoon, A Troop. One of its tanks was fording a river and went into a shell hole sinking below the turret. Later, I worked with CPT Meaders and Top Walker to draft a new citation and inducted the tank crew into the "Mysterious and Sacred order of the Yellow Submarine". By then hardly anybody was left in 1st Platoon who remembered the great river crossing, but we kept the tradition alive.

Four hours later we were back at Con Thien. Because of my date of rank, I was the senior lieutenant in the TOC, and therefor officially Assistant S3. Mostly I supervised radio operations, relayed messages, and wrote plans. I was also responsible for setting up briefings and reporting on the plans and operations portion of briefings.

Three additional lieutenants worked with me. Two duty officers split twenty-four hours daily on the radios while an additional liaison officer spent most of his time running back and forth to Brigade HQ. I did not get out of the TOC very much. Everyone lived underground. There were so many of us underground, so the story went, that the rats had to build their own bunkers.

We rarely experienced a dull moment at Con Tien. During our first two days there we had contact. On the first day a Marine reconnaissance patrol called for help and we sent a troop and called in air strikes in their support that netted 15 NVA KIA. A Troop followed up the next day by searching the area. They did not find anything, but one ACAV ran afoul of a mine and blew up while an RPG hit one of their tanks resulting in three wounded, none seriously. A couple of days later Fire Base A4 to our south reported being probed around sunset by eight to ten NVA. The next morning one of our patrols went into an area east of A4 and found a squad size base but drew no contact. This typified the cat and mouse nature of life on the DMZ.

On the evening of 18 April, our C Troop minus one platoon, accompanied by two platoons of C Company, 1st Battalion, 9th Marine Regiment, operating about two kilometers northwest of Con Thien, prepared to go into their night defensive positions. Shortly after dark, C Troop (-) received heavy mortar fire followed by RPG fire from close range on the north side of their perimeter hitting seven of the tracks inflicting heavy casualties. The troop commander, artillery forward observer and one platoon sergeant were wounded and both medics killed. Enemy sappers then moved through the gap in the northern defense perimeter throwing satchel charges at and into the rear of tracks to the south. Quick action by 1LT Richard Brawn (a classmate) who took command and maneuvered his track to close the gap in the northern side of the perimeter stabilized the situation. Additionally, the artillery radioman regained contact with the Squadron artillery liaison enabling supporting artillery units to adjust fire close to the perimeter and call for illumination fire, Puff the Magic Dragon and finally medivac helicopters.

We in the TOC did what we could to coordinate the responses to the action dispatching A Troop (-) to the battle site to reinforce C Troop (-) and flush out and destroy any lingering NVA in the area. A total of eleven members of C Troop were killed, twenty-three wounded and twelve out of twenty-one tracks hit, six a total loss as result of the action.

On the morning of April 19, 3/5 Cavalry, accompanied by elements of 1/9 Marines and 5th Mechanized Infantry Brigade conducted a search of the battle site. They found seven dead NVA bringing the total enemy KIA to thirteen. They also found an enemy bunker within 300 meters of C Troop's night defensive position and individual bunkers within the north side of the perimeter. Further analysis revealed that C Troop had not complied fully with Squadron SOP in preparing its NDP. Specifically, they did not conduct a dismounted search of the immediate area. Neither did they relocate their position prior to dark enabling the enemy to thoroughly scout the site and make the best preparations for the attack. C Troop also failed to dismount M60 machine guns and dig them in between their ACAVs and tanks.[12]

The battle at Nui Tot Mon as it came to be known proved to be the worst drubbing 3/5 Cavalry had since Tet '68. We in Squadron HQ were dazed and confused. It was not the same as after a contact of your own in which you lost men of your own. That left a far more intense feeling that lingers for years. And with it comes the feeling of knowing that you were whipped. It is such a helpless feeling to be in the command center hearing it on the radio and knowing that the voice on the other end is a friend. You call in the artillery and air strikes and call for other units to maneuver and assist and in the end call for the medivac. It

---

[12] Memo, LTC Carpenter to CO, 1st BDE, 5th ID (MECH), 23 Apr 1969; Combat After Action Report, CO, 1st BDE, 5th ID (MECH) to CO, US Army Vietnam, 26 Apr 1969.

is an equally helpless feeling having someone call for help and having to tell them it is on the way, just ten minutes out and to hold on. I had been on the other end too, waiting for the air strike. The difference was we came out ahead then.

What a morbid way of deciding who wins or loses by counting bodies and going through the pockets of the dead looking for documents or letters to get information about who they were. There were times when I was still in the field and hungry that I used to step back and look at myself and wonder what was happening to me. I still do not really know. One can become immersed in the mechanics of one's job, I guess.

Duty in the TOC was not frantic all the time. When none of the line troops were in the field, we found other things to do with the extra time on our hands. For example, I went back and forth with Jo about wedding plans and my orders to Germany. Both subjects set me up for a lot of ribbing. COL Carpenter and MAJ Krawciw frequently asked how the plans were going. MAJ K often prefaced his remarks with, "Oh to be young again and in love." Even Jim Bursitis got into the act on one of his visits to the TOC, asking if Jo was "Ranger qualified?" implying that any army wife should be. The CO gave advice on living and serving in Germany that he hoped might allay Jo's concerns about going on an overseas assignment straight after the wedding.

We did not stay long at Con Thien after the battle at Nui Tot Mon.

The 5th Mech sent the squadron's line troops on a reconnaissance in force through the Ruong Ruong Valley that ran northwest to southeast from Keh Sanh to Quang Tri. It represented a high-speed avenue of approach from Laos to the coast for an NVA force attempting to turn the flank of the DMZ. In the Spring of 1969 3/5 Cavalry found no sign of an enemy presence in the Ruong Ruong. Three years later, at the start of its April Offensive against South Vietnam, the NVA utilized the same approach to invade northern Quang Tri province.

I joined the TOC on the move through the Ruong Ruong only briefly. MAJ K sent me back to Camp Evans with a draft of the Squadron's Quarterly Report with instructions to complete it and prepare it to go to division. At the same time, he told me that he and the CO had decided to move me over to the S2 (Intelligence) position as that had recently become vacant.

While at Evans I went back to A Troop for a visit with some of the men in the Troop headquarters platoon with whom I worked closely during my time as XO. As I approached the troop area wearing clean and freshly pressed fatigues, I perceived a difference in how the men responded to me. The old familiarity that sustained us was now gone. No longer one of them, I was now part of the other "them" to be viewed with suspicion as in "what is he doing here?" That invisible bond that holds soldiers who shared the highs and lows of war together was broken, and it could not be reforged.[13]

My comings and goings between Wunder Beach, Camp Evans and DaNang took me through Hue several times, but never into the old imperial citadel. While I was at Evans still working on the quarterly report, I took advantage of the opportunity to go back to Hue for another look. That was not as easy as it sounds, because Hue, like all South Vietnamese cities and towns, was off limits to U.S. personnel except for official business which did not include sightseeing. Another officer and I concocted a scheme to get by the prohibition. We gathered up a map of the city, stamped it SECRET, got a measuring tape and a twelve-foot stick, commandeered a jeep, and drove to the city.

The ancient city is walled and surrounded by a moat. Entry to the walled city, once the residence of the imperial household, was via gated bridges at several points along the walls. We pulled up to the nearest entry point and proceeded to measure the width and length of the bridge and then the width, height and depth of the gate. We then wrote the figures down in a notebook, also marked SECRET, noted its location on the map and finished up taking pictures from several angles. Then we moved on to the next entry point.

At our third stop the Military Police caught up with us, reminded us about the city's off-limits status and asked us what we were doing. I introduced myself as the S2 of the 3rd Squadron, 5th Cavalry and explained that the Cav had a secondary mission to react to the city in an emergency. To prepare for that mission we needed to classify the bridges and know the dimensions of the bridges, gates and major through streets in the city for our tanks and ACAVs. We were photographing key entry points, streets and landmarks for briefing purposes so commanders and platoon leaders who would execute any reaction would know a little about what to expect. Thereafter we had a personal MP escort to clear traffic as we continued our "mission" and got the grand tour of the ancient city.

On April 30, MAJ K picked up my work on the quarterly report and headed for Dong Tam. The next day I returned to the forward command post and began my real work as S2.

---

[13] A good example of this phenomenon can be found in Farley Mowat's memoir of his WWII service in the Canadian Army, *And No Birds Sang*, Atlantic Monthly Press (1979). See esp. pp. 123-124.

Chapter Fourteen
Into the A Shau and Home

With the end of the Ruong Ruong operation, the Squadron reverted to operational control (OPCON) of the 3rd BDE, 101st Airborne Division and returned to Camp Evans. A week of stand down for maintenance and refitting prepared it for a new mission aimed at conducting a reconnaissance in force into the A Shau Valley to clear it of NVA/VC forces and block the Ho Chi Minh Trail.

The concept of the operation called for three infantry battalions of the 101st to enter the valley by helicopter assault supported by an artillery battalion and the 3rd of the 5th Cavalry moving overland along QL547 from Hue to the southern entrance of the A Shau. A company of engineers accompanied the 3/5 Cavalry to clear obstacles and improve the highway for logistical transportation. My initial task was to prepare the INTSUM (Intelligence Summary). This involved synthesizing information covering the period of the operation including, summarizing the enemy situation around the area of operations, enemy strengths, capabilities, and limitations as well as weather and terrain characteristics. Before and during the operation, I would conduct first and last light aerial reconnaissance flights along the route to keep track of the progress. In preparation I spent much of my time moving back and forth between Brigade and Division headquarters, visiting my counterparts in other battalions and flying over the area we would be moving through to glean as much as I could about the territory we would be operating in.

The evening before we moved out, several of us, mostly A Troop alumni and current officers hosted a party with some doctors, nurses and orderlies from the 18th Surgical Hospital. We, almost to a man, sported moustaches which became the subject of much comment. This led to a discussion of cavalry customs and traditions and badly sung renditions of cavalry songs. My moustache, now neatly trimmed, along with my adherence to cavalry customs and traditions, continued to draw attention.

Movement south on QL1 from Evans to Hue and then west on QL547 to FSB Bastogne went smoothly. The squadron had been that way before just after it moved to northern I Corps in March 1968. Then, A Troop under OPCON to 101st Air Cavalry Division, was pushing its way up QL547 in pursuit of NVA troops retreating from Hue. Along the way, they supported improvements to the route as well as construction of a series of fire bases for artillery units that could fire into the A Shau. I heard many tales of battles fought along QL547 while I was a platoon leader in A Troop.

Now, we moved well beyond Bastogne toward the entrance to the valley itself. As we did so, we sent scouts up the draws emptying into the QL547 valley. On more than one occasion they found well camouflaged Chinese and Russian trucks left behind by retreating NVA forces the previous year. Some were still fueled, and our mechanics succeeded in starting some. We also found a Soviet 85mm gun and some ammunition in one of the draws.

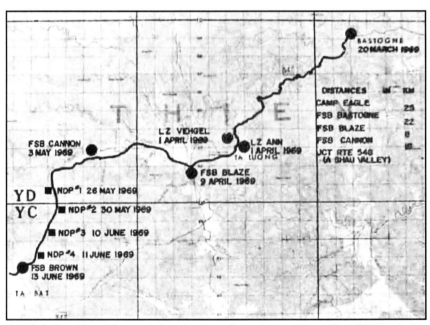

MAP 4 - Into the Ashaw, 1969. 547, The Ashaw Expressway. The KSYU' A Publication of Engineer Troops Vietnam, Fall 1969. This map depicts the Area of Operations of the 59th Land Clearing Company as supported by 3rd Squadron 5 Cavalry as it reopened QL 547 into the Ashaw between March and July 1969.

Movement west was governed by the engineers' slow progress at widening and improving the road. Almost every day, late afternoon thunderstorms deluged the area wiping out half of the day's work.[14]

Eventually we reached the entrance to the A Shau. The Squadron set up its headquarters and TOC at FSB Blaze that overlooked the intersection of QL547 and QL548 which ran north to south through the A Shau. The line troops rotated providing security to QL547, the fire bases and the engineers as they continued to punch through the rugged terrain and link up the two routes. Today both QL547 and QL548 are all-weather highways. QL548 is appropriately named the Ho Chi Minh Highway.

FSB Blaze Ashaw Valley

3rd Brigade 101st Airborne (Airmobile)Division did not wait for the engineers to complete linking highways QL547 and QL548. On May 10 three Infantry battalions of the brigade conducted airmobile combat assaults into the valley and began the planned reconnaissance in force. Initially the Infantry ex-

---

[14] The task of extending QL547 fell to the 59th Land Clearing Company. See "547 The A Shau Expressway" by First Lieutenant J. P. Donahu in *The KYSU' A Quarterly Publication of Engineer Troops Vietnam* Vol. 1, No. 3 pp. 6-9.

perienced little opposition as they advanced, but that changed as the NVA drew them into a series of preplanned positions including trenches and bunkers on the slopes of increasingly mountainous terrain. As American casualties mounted, additional battalions were committed to the fight ending with a full-scale assault on the mountain itself. U.S. losses totaled seventy-two killed, 400-plus wounded and seven missing. Enemy killed based on a body count of 630 was estimated to be much higher. The NVA claimed 1500 killed and wounded.[15] We stood by helplessly monitoring the battle and carrying litters of wounded that came through the aid station adjacent to our TOC to be triaged and moved on for further care.

Meanwhile, we received an alert that we were going to be visited by a VIP. The operation in the A Shaw, now dubbed the Battle of Hamburger Hill had sparked considerable public outcry at home inviting congressional hearings. The rumor quickly spread that the VIP was Secretary of Defense Melvin Laird, or possibly Secretary of State William Rogers. Talk about a Chinese fire drill. The first thing that happened was that brigade headquarters called to inform us what we needed to do in preparation for the visit. Our space at Blaze needed sprucing up. We needed to be spruced up. We would be getting a portable shower unit to help with that. We needed to have coffee and pastry for the visitors. We had to prepare briefing charts. And, oh by the way, the division commander would be stopping by before the visit to inspect our preparations. The event was scheduled for the afternoon of May 18.

While we in the TOC scurried around making our preparations, others in the squadron headquarters did what they could to make the area look more presentable. They cleared up the area around the helicopter landing pad and raked the dirt and rocks leading to the TOC. The only thing we lacked was paint for the rocks.[16] The portable shower unit arrived, and we began running the troops through it as fast as we could. Then the division commander, Major General Melvin Zais arrived and proceeded to come through the TOC accompanied by Colonel Carpenter. When he got to my station, he took one look at me and thrust his face into mine growling, "Is that a moustache? Airborne troopers don't wear moustaches!" "Sir, I'm Cavalry." I replied proudly, and

---

[15] "The Battle of Hamburger Hill," Wikipedia, April 9, 2021.
[16] Preparing for VIP visits in combat zones is one of the absurdities of war. I often wondered how common this practice was in previous conflicts. For example, did any VIPs visit the 101 Airborne Division at the real town of Bastogne while it was surrounded during the Battle of the Bulge in 1944?

he moved on in a huff. Later, Colonel Carpenter put me at ease with words to affect that cavalrymen had been wearing moustaches a hundred years before there were airplanes for airborne troopers to jump out of. I could have hugged him.

Later in the day, the weather turned sour and thunderstorms threatened. Brigade informed us that the visit was cancelled. Two hours later brigade called back to say the visit was back on. This continued for two days. The visit was on again, off again depending on the severity of weather. Finally, on May 18, brigade told us that the visit was on after the rain. Less than an hour later they called again to tell us it was off. The last thing we heard, later still in the afternoon, was that the visit *might* be on. It never happened. But at least we got a shower out of it.[17]

Things settled down after the brouhaha over the VIP visit. We never did learn who the VIP was. The squadron settled back into its routine of securing QL547, escorting convoys from Hue to Bastogne and securing Blaze while the engineers tried to complete the link between QL547 and QL548. I resumed my daily aerial reconnaissance of our area of operations. As May waned, we began to get indications that an attack on our position might be pending. The brigade S2 advised us that "a usually reliable source" informed them that a fire base on QL547 housing 175mm cannons had been thoroughly scouted, including the location of bunkers, and "that an attack can be expected at any time." In turn, I advised all 3/5 Cavalry troops and C/2-34 Armor plus artillery and engineer units in the area that they should prepare for possible attacks on their night defensive positions and sniping and harassing fire on their movements during the day. That attack, when it came, was directed at Bastogne resulting in ten NVA killed and numerous weapons and other equipment seized, compared to three U.S. KIAs, sixteen wounded and four trucks destroyed.[18]

By that time, I was already gone. My DROS of June 9, had approached so rapidly that I could think of little else. Nevertheless, I stayed on task right until my last night in the field. That night, May 31, I was jumpy. Most of us in the TOC slept on the roof because it was too hot and stuffy inside. By then the expected attack on our position so dominated my thoughts that I bedded down armed to the teeth. I took a lot of ribbing from the rest of the

---

[17] HQ 3rd Squadron, 5th Cavalry, S3, Duty Officers Log, 16, 18 May '69, passim.
[18] Memorandum for CO, 3rd Brigade, 101st Abn Div (Airmobile) from CO, 3rd Squadron, 5th Cavalry, 9 June 1969, p. 1.

guys over it. Not so long ago I could distinguish between out-going and incoming artillery fire and easily sleep through the former. Now I hardly slept. In the morning I said my goodbyes to my friends in the TOC and A Troop and flew back to Evans to out process. I wrote my last letters home to my parents and Jo. She and I had been exchanging letters regularly since 1965. It seemed strange knowing that this would likely be the last letter I ever addressed to Miss Johana Doyle.

Years later, I learned that the engineers broke into the Ashaw in June. This enabled the Cavalry to move into the valley, where it conducted armored and armored cavalry operations dominating North Vietnamese units there. That had been the original plan. But time and larger events changed plans. By mid-June with the withdrawal of the Marines from the DMZ, the 101st Division with 3/5 Cavalry relocated to the north. U.S. forces never returned to the Ashaw.

I have no memory of leaving Camp Evans, how or where I went to get my flight home. I do remember that it was not Saigon and that several of my West Point classmates were on the same flight home. One of them and I made a point of promoting ourselves to captain as we crossed the international date line somewhere over the Pacific Ocean.[19]

We landed at Seattle-Tacoma airport. Since it was a charter flight from Vietnam, we had no trouble clearing customs and boarder control. An army reception team clearly practiced in its task briefed us, told us where we could change into our khaki summer uniforms, where to retrieve our baggage and how to find commercial flights to our final destinations. I quickly shed my tropical fatigues, donned my khakis, and headed for the United Airlines reservations desk. Based on my orders the agent issued me a military standby ticket to Boston and directed me to the boarding area. Several returning GIs and a couple of civilians preceded me in the standby waiting area. We nervously watched as the full-fare passengers boarded the plane. It quickly became obvious that the flight would not be full, and the boarding agent turned his attention to us standbys. He boarded the civilians first without regard to our order in the standby queue. Then he proceeded to board all the military standby passengers in First Class! The flight attendants were waiting for us. They welcomed us to First Class and started making a fuss over us before the

---

[19] Rank came quickly in those days. First lieutenants made captain in twenty-four months from date of commissioning. We were known as shake and bake captains.

plane left the gate. All through the flight they plied us with food and drink. I have flown First Class a few times since, but the memory of that flight home sticks in my mind as one of the best.

I changed planes in Chicago and lost my First-Class status. The last leg of the trip home passed uneventfully. My whole family and Jo met me at Logan Airport. The other GIs and I moved through the airport not greeted as baby killers or with catcalls. Nobody spit at us. This was a far cry from what we had been led to expect. I found It hard to believe that less than two weeks before I had been flying first and last light visual reconnaissance missions over the A Shau Valley.

Less than two weeks later, Jo and I married in Worcester.

Epilogue

I did not talk much about Vietnam at first. The two most common questions I got were, "How was it?" and "How is it going?" I rarely answered the former. Those who knew me understood that I had been wounded twice, lost a couple of my soldiers to friendly fire, and received three medals for bravery. Relatively speaking there was nothing special to tell. As to my assessment of how things were going, at first, I gave glowing reports that we were winning in Vietnam. I drew on my experience along QL1 as a metaphor. When I arrived in June 1968, we were literally fighting the enemy on the beach east of the main north-south route in the country. When I left a year later, we were fighting well to the west along the Cambodian border. More important, Highway 1 itself had changed for the better. By the end of my tour, it was paved from Danang to just below the DMZ at Dong Ha. Moreover, commerce was thriving, and the local schools were open on a regular basis. All in all, things seemed to be going in a positive direction. We were even beginning to withdraw American troops and turning the war back to the Vietnamese. QL1 had become my Congo River in Joseph Conrad's *Heart of Darkness*, but the outcome was more favorable.

From 1969 to 1971, my thoughts about Vietnam took a back seat to the challenges I faced as an Armor company commander and then as the adjutant of a tank battalion in Germany. When I returned to the United States to attend further training as a combat arms officer in 1971, I confronted the probability that we were losing the war in Vietnam. The North Vietnam "Easter Offensive" in April 1972 unraveled any gains we had achieved to that point. The fact that the NVA's offensive took control of the two northern provinces of South Vietnam I was most familiar with made a big impression on me. During my graduate studies at Brown University and subsequent teaching assignment at West Point, I studied the war in detail. Eventually, I reached the conclusion that our involvement in the war and our prosecution of it had been wrongheaded from the start. The single book that most shaped my thinking on the subject was Kai Bird's study of the Bundy brothers, *The Color of Truth* (1998). In it, Bird made the case that the United States' national command authority concluded that the war was unwinnable as early as 1965. That was fully two years before I and everyone I served with in that war went there, and everyone I knew who died there. I felt totally betrayed.[20]

Back to the Beach

I went back to Vietnam in September 2010, after forty-two years. Even before I left in 1969, I knew I would return someday.

The occasion was serendipitous. My youngest daughter, Anne, had left her well-paying, secure job in San Francisco to "find herself" and chose Southeast Asia as her venue. To appease me and her mother, she suggested that I join her during the Vietnam leg of her travels to show her "my part" of the country.

So, there she and I were on a bus from Phnom Penh, Cambodia to Ho Chi Minh City (a.k.a. Saigon). When we arrived at the border, I felt a surge of anxiety. Passing out of Cambodia was perfunctory, going into Vietnam intimidating. The frontier crossing point was a military installation; a huge red flag emblazoned with a yellow star, waved lazily in the hot, heavy air, signs prohibiting photographs abounded and grim-faced immigration and customs officials barked instructions ordering us off the bus and into a large waiting hall. Cambodians and Vietnamese were herded one way, the rest of us another. The border guards checked our bags, took our passports, and left us standing in an unadorned room with no seats. Shortly, they returned and began calling people by surname and country. Anne and I were called last. She went through quickly. I found myself standing before a senior officer judging by his age and

---

[20] Kai Bird, *The Color of Truth. McGeorge Bundy and William Bundy: Brothers in Arms.* Simon & Schuster (1998). More damning is H.R. McMaster. *Dereliction of Duty: Lyndon Johnson, Robert McNamara, The Joint Chiefs of Staff and the Lies that led to Vietnam.* Harper Collins (1997).

rank (lieutenant colonel, I guessed). He scrutinized my passport and visa, looked me up, looked me down, looked back to my passport, stamped me in and returned it. "Welcome back," he said with a broad smile.

I had spent little time in Saigon. The new Ho Chi Minh City towers over old Saigon. It is crowded, loud, jammed with traffic, peddlers and street vendors who aggressively hustle for the tourist dollar. We stayed about a day and a half and took a night bus toward Hue. It is just as well that we traveled at night. Vietnamese drivers abide by no discernable rules-of-the-road. Larger vehicles assert the right-of-way by passing on the right or left and announcing their presence with their horns. Narrow bridges, blind curves and steep, winding mountainous stretches do not deter the aggressive drivers. At least at night passengers are spared the scarier parts of the trip.

We approached Hue via Da Nang two mornings later. Da Nang is a city on the move. To its south new beachside resorts are blossoming as fast as they can be built. In the city itself prominent billboards advertise old resorts built by the French and Americans like China Beach and Marble Mountain. A new, modern tunnel sped us under Hai Van Pass and past more newly constructed beach resorts on the way to Hue. Though I had driven between Danang and Hue several times the landscape was unfamiliar. Stretches of QL1 that once were cleared of vegetation that could conceal snipers have now grown up. Motor bikes, pickup trucks and mini-vans, long haul trucks and buses, even occasional personal automobiles compete for the highway.

Our route into Hue took us past the Notre Dame Cathedral, a fusion of French and Asian architecture that was heavily damaged in the battle for Hue during Tet '68. From there we took a circuitous path along Le Loi Street on the south bank of the Perfume River. Across the river I could see the flag of the SRV flying over the Citadel of the old Imperial City. After several days in the country where the flag, along with giant pictures of Ho Chi Minh, are ubiquitous, it no longer intimidated me. We spent the rest of the day exploring the city south of the river.

Prior to leaving home, I had made contact with the director of an NGO based in Dong Ha who offered to help me find a reliable driver and interpreter that could help us explore the area I'd spent most of my time back in '68 and '69. When that fell through, an alternative presented itself on the bus from Saigon in the form of a casual relationship that turned into a genuine friendship. Long Ngoc Dang was born in Hue. He served in the Army of the Republic of

Vietnam (ARVN) as an interpreter for the U.S. Army Quartermaster Corp at the Long Bien depot near Saigon. When the North triumphed in 1975, he and his family escaped and eventually found their way to the United States. He was returning to visit relatives in Hue where, it turned out, his nephew was a registered tour guide. Working with Long and his nephew we secured the needed driver and interpreter. Over the ritual coffee that precedes any business transaction in Vietnam, Anne and I, overseen by Long, laid out my old 1:50,000 maps and showed our prospective team where we wanted to go.

We left the next day. The drive took us north on Route QL1 past Hue. QL1, like the sections we had been on earlier, was a definite improvement over what I remembered. It is paved from Saigon to Hanoi, with modern truck stops and tourist facilities on the outskirts of most major towns. Newly constructed schools, military barracks, commercial and industrial facilities line the highway between towns. Within town limits markets, mixed-use residential and commercial stores, repair facilities and restaurants predominate. In other words, it is the strip-malling of QL1. Peddlers and kids mob buses and cars to sell their wares or beg. The people were all remarkably familiar; the landscape was not.

I had expected, hoped, to see the places I soldiered as an armored cavalry platoon leader. Of course, I knew they would be different, but I assumed they would be recognizable. Some were, most were not. I especially wanted to see those places we had fought; Binh An, where our cavalry squadron and battalions from the 1st Cavalry Division annihilated a battalion of some 300 North Vietnamese Army troops. Van Phong, where in a pitched battle with another NVA unit my Platoon Sergeant Clarence Fulton and another of my men, Donald Sizemore, were killed by friendly fire, and Bac Ta, where, two days later, we caught up with the same NVA unit and killed or captured its remaining soldiers. I most wanted to walk again on the road from Hai Lang to Hoi Yen (known to us as LZ Hard Core), where on my first night as a platoon leader one of my armored cavalry assault vehicles was blown up by a command detonated mine, wounding all four crewmen. I wanted to walk there again. It was my baptism by fire.

The drive north took about an hour. I followed our progress on my old maps while Tran Sam, our interpreter, pointed out landmarks and Anne peppered me with questions like, "What's that place?" and "What happened there?" Sometimes I answered, sometimes Sam did. He pointed out what looked like a sand and gravel plant off to the west. "That was LZ Nancy, now it's a cement factory," he said, referring to a former base camp. Sure enough it was right where it was supposed to be, according to my map.

About 40 km. on, at Phong Dien, we turned west off the highway and headed up a paved road into what looked like an industrial park in waiting. This, Sam told us, was the site of Camp Evans, my squadron's base camp from November 1968 to mid-1969. Once home to a brigade of the 1st Cavalry Division and later the 101st Airborne Division, it is now devoid of human habitation. The trace of the main runway was plainly visible as were some partially filled in revetments, but nothing else. Moving on we came to My Chan, a market town at the confluence of the My Chan and O Giang rivers and the site where the ARVN made its stand against the NVA onslaught during the Easter Offensive of 1972. We hung a right and drove east along the river until we intersected Route 555, the "Street Without Joy" immortalized by Bernard Fall in his book by the same name. This would have been impossible back in the day. Secondary roads were unpaved then, rivers, streams and canals were not bridged, and few were fordable. Now we made the drive in about an hour. Much has changed.

"The Street," clearly marked on my map, had been the epicenter of my squadron's combat operations from June until November 1968. Main force NVA units supported by local VC remained in the area after being driven out of Hue. It had been our mission to root them out and restore control to the South Vietnamese government. But everything looked totally unfamiliar to me.

According to Sam, most of the villages, roads and other infrastructure had been thoroughly rubbled during the fighting in 1972. The population was evacuated to camps south of Hue, and the unified government that took over in 1975 did not let the refugees return until the early to mid-1980s after the rubble and unexploded ordnance had been cleared from previously populated areas. Only then could the rural peasants begin to rebuild and bring the land back under cultivation. Even today farmers and children frequently fall victim to dud rounds and old booby traps (we call them IEDs now). But rebuild they did!

Today rice remains the primary crop of Quang Tri province, but that is not all. Areas previously unfarmed now boast rubber and banana plantations, and aquaculture, in the form of shrimp farms, is taking hold. The peasants who work the rice paddies, plantations and aquaculture ventures now raise duck and cattle for their own use and market. They also rebuilt the villages, roads, bridges and agricultural infrastructure. All the secondary and tertiary roads are paved. Irrigation canals are concrete; major irrigation canals are covered to prevent erosion and evaporation, canals feeding individual paddies are lined. Flood control projects abound, though the region continues to suffer major inundations during typhoon season. In October, a month after we left Vietnam, flash floods spawned by Typhoon Megi swept coastal central Vietnam destroying over 250,000 homes and threatening the rice crop.

Beyond infrastructure the people of Quang Tri Province rebuilt their villages as well. Today one is hard pressed to find homes built of woven mat walls and thatched roofs on dirt floors. Almost all homes in peasant villages are built on cement slabs. The two story, pastel-colored residential buildings are made of concrete blocks faced with stucco or tile and have tile roofs. Most have running water and electricity; satellite dishes are not uncommon. Cars and motor bikes are everywhere. Buddhist temples and Christian, mostly Catholic, churches and schools have also been rebuilt. But the places I wanted to see again are not there. The only way I knew where I was in my former area of operations along "The Street" was by following our progress on my map. I was not expecting manicured battlefields like Gettysburg or The Somme. But I was expecting something to evoke memories of those battles and the men who died in them.

The place names, Hai Lang, Hoi Yen (LZ Hard Core), My Thuy (Wunder Beach), and the battle fields at Binh An, Van Phong and Bac Ta are still there, but it is not the same. Just once, at a crossroad bisecting some fallow rice paddies at Van Phong did I sense something vaguely familiar. The villages are rebuilt better than I could have imagined. Who would have thought Binh An could be rebuilt after the way we leveled it? There is even a monument commemorating the North Vietnamese killed there. The one thing that remains unchanged is "The Beach." What we knew as Wunder Beach, our base camp on the Tonkin Gulf while we worked to clear and pacify "The Street" is the same, pristine and beautiful as ever. The military base and port facility that the U.S. built there is gone of course. But "The Beach" remains. The water is warm, and slash pines and palms provide welcome shade on hot sunny days. We took a brief swim, and I regaled Anne and Sam our driver, of the fun times we had there on the few occasions we spent "inside the wire" of Wunder Beach forgetting the war.

Fishermen had reclaimed the Beach and the village that we displaced in 1968. Their boats, narrow wooden, shallow draft vessels with high prows and sterns, seem the same, though some of the boats have motors. A few hundred meters back from the water's edge the fishermen and their families live in modern villages much like those the farming peasants live in. Today, instead of hiking across the desert-like expanse of sand dunes and scrub brush between the beach and the towns along QL1 they carry their catch to market in trucks or on motorbikes.

We left the beach and travelled north on a road that was not even a path on my map from 1968, crossed the Qua Viet River and picked up QL9 at Dong Ha. Heading west on QL9 that leads to Cam Lo, the "Rock Pile," Khe Sanh (now a minor tourist trap), and eventually crossing into Laos we stopped at the national military cemetery at Truong Son. It contains the complete and partial remains of thousands of Vietnamese "heroes and martyrs" who died in and around the former DMZ largely at our hands. It reminded me of the vast WWI French military cemetery at Verdun, where every identifiable body has an individual grave, and the unidentifiable partial remains and scraps of bones of countless unknowns lie in an ossuary for pilgrims to view. Like all military cemeteries Truong Son left me feeling empty and wondering. After witnessing how far the peasants of Quang Tri Province have come since the end of the war it is hard to avoid the thought that they could have come so much further had they been left alone. Likewise, it is hard to avoid thinking what those NVA and VC dead might have accomplished, as we too continue to mourn, honor and wonder what our own brothers who died in that wasteful adventure might have done.

The day was slipping away when we reached Con Thien, one of the strong points of our defensive line below the DMZ. It served as our Squadron's Tactical Operations Center during the early months of 1969 when we took it over from the Marines. I remembered a WWI-like trench, bunker and barbed wire complex that afforded a broad view of the north as well as the hills and valleys east and west of the position. Perhaps I could catch a glimpse of the area Tom Emerson fell before darkness overtook us. We trudged to the top only to find it overgrown with second growth timber, elephant grass and wild banana trees. Nature has reclaimed it. There are no signs of the trenches or bunkers. Only

LONG AGO AND FAR AWAY • 95

some barbed wire remains reused to protect a plantation of rubber trees on the lower slope of the hill. On the way down we got caught up in a swathe of wait-a-minute vines that slashed at our ankles.

Last stop was at the Hien Loung Bridge over the Ben Hai River that once served as the DMZ between North and South Vietnam. Again, a huge flag waves atop a citadel-like base on the northern side of the river. On the other side is a victory monument honoring both the soldiers and civilians who manned and supported the defenses of the north from 1954 to 1972. A heroic statue of Ho Chi Minh (all the statues of Ho are heroic) welcomes visitors to an adjacent museum. But it was getting dark, starting to rain, and I was very, very tired. We rode back to Hue in silence.

Glossary

ACAV – Armored Cavalry Assault Vehicle

ARA – Arial Rocket Artillery fired by helicopter.

ARVN – Army of the Republic of Vietnam

ASP – Ammunition Storage Point

AVLB – Armored Vehicle Launched Bridge

Charlie – Nickname for Vietcong soldier

DMZ – Demilitarized Zone between North and South Vietnam

DROS – Date of Return from Overseas

Gook – Derogatory, racist name for any Southeast Asian

Grunt – Infantry soldier

LZ – Landing Zone

FSB – Fire Support Base

NCO – Non-Commissioned Officer, Sargent

NDP – Night Defensive Position

NVA – North Vietnam Army

RF/PF – Regional Forces/Popular Forces – South Vietnamese Militia, equivalent to National Guard or local Reserve

RPG – Rocket Propelled Grenade – shoulder fired anti-tank or personnel rocket used by NVA/VC

Snake & Nape – 250-pound high drag bomb (Snake) and 500-pound Napalm bomb used in support of ground forces in Vietnam.

Thud – Tactical Air Force fighter/bomber, F105 Thunderchief

Track – Any tracked vehicle. Tank, ACAV, self-propelled Artillery, recovery vehicle

TC – Track Commander

TOC – Tactical Operations Center

VC – Viet Cong. Also, Victor Charlie

Appendix I
NVA/VC Propaganda

> - G.I.S! Refuse to obey the order of killing, burning, robbing, destroying the crops of Vietnam people.
> - Wait to be captured of cross over to the Ranks of the south Vietnam liberation army and be well treated.

Appendix II
Yellow Submarine Certificate

DEPARTMENT OF THE ARMY
HEADQUARTERS 1ST PLATOON
TROOP A
3RD SQUADRON 5TH CAVALRY
APO SAN FRANCISCO 96370

SPECIAL ORDER   15 September 1968
NUMBER 1

HEAR YEE, HEAR YEA

Attention to orders all who call themselves Cavalry

1. Wherefore that on the 16th Day of August in the year of our Lord One Thousand Nine Hundred Sixty eight the 1st Platoon of A Troop 3rd Squadron 5th United States Cavalry did attempt to cross the O Lau river at the village of Ly Chanh.

2. Wherefore that in the honest attempt at crossing said river near said village on said date The 13, 14 and 15 ACAVS did founder and sink to the deep six.

3. Wherefore the crews of said ACAVS which dove into said river near said village on said date did distinguish themselves in their valiant but vain attempts to surface.

4. Wherefore the said crews of said vehicles which dove into said river near said village on said date were recovery of same have now decorated their vehicles with the sacred symbol of the yellow submarine.

5. Therefore on this the 15th day of September year of our Lord 1968 by the powers conferred upon us by Him, Neptune and his Prime Minister David Jones do declare the following Yellow Submariners and admit them into said society with all rights and privileges.

    1LT Miguel A. Robles 13TU
    PFC Casey J. Hoffman 13O
    PFC O___ F. _____ 13O
    PFC Montgomery J. Maser 13O
    PFC Alvin D. _____ 11D
    PFC Tommy L. Justice 11D
    PFC Thomas J. Burke 11D
    SP4 Howard V. Pitts 13TU
    SP5 Roger D. Ward 15D
    SP5 Chad ___ ___ L. Riddle 15D
    SP5 L___ L___ D. Porter 15D

                        ROBERT K. GRIFFITH Jr.
                        1LT Armor
                        Platoon Leader

LONG AGO AND FAR AWAY • 101

Printed in the USA
CPSIA information can be obtained
at www.ICGtesting.com
CBHW040053120924
14111CB00030B/144